WORLD AS LOVER, WORLD AS SELF

I should not like to have the bodhisattva think this kind of work hard to achieve and hard to plan out. If he did, there are beings beyond calculation, and he will not be able to benefit them. Let him on the contrary consider the work easy and pleasant, thinking they were all his mother and father and children, for this is the way to benefit all beings whose number is beyond calculation.

—*The Perfection of Wisdom in 8,000 Lines*

WORLD AS LOVER
WORLD AS SELF

COURAGE FOR GLOBAL JUSTICE
AND ECOLOGICAL RENEWAL

Joanna Macy

**PARALLAX
PRESS**

BERKELEY, CALIFORNIA

PARALLAX PRESS
P.O. BOX 7355, BERKELEY, CALIFORNIA 94707
www.parallax.org

Parallax Press is the publishing division of Unified Buddhist Church, Inc.
Copyright © 2007 by Joanna Macy
All Rights Reserved.

Textual references and permissions appear at the end of the book.
Cover design by Grégoire Vion.
Text design by Gopa & Ted2, Inc.

Library of Congress Cataloging-in-Publication Data

Macy, Joanna, 1929-
  World as lover, world as self : courage for global justice and ecological renewal / by Joanna Macy.
     p. cm.
  Includes bibliographical references.
  ISBN-13: 978-1-888375-71-8
  1. Buddhism—Social aspects. 2. Human ecology—Philosophy.
3. System theory. I. Title.
  BQ4570.S6M33 2007
  294.3'42—dc22

                              2007022262

7 8 / 17 16

Contents

FOREWORD

ON LABOR DAY WEEKEND 2006, a small band of concerned citizens took a long walk together to raise issues of climate change. They started in Robert Frost's birth place in Vermont and walked for five days to Burlington City Hall. Along the way they talked about our world and the world they want for their children. Each day more people joined the group until a thousand people were gathered at Battery Park. One by one, the political candidates of both parties for all the major offices came up to the stage and signed our climate pledge.

All of us in that crowd knew the world was in unprecedented danger from global overheating. Yet here we were, turning our despair into hope, our paralysis into action. As we engaged the impossible koan of climate change, we were planting seeds of faith and courage for the long haul. We were responding to the call to act on behalf of the larger whole, the miracle that is this earth our home. We were taking up the activist's journey, each step moved by urgency but also fierce love.

In this new revision of Joanna Macy's long beloved volume, *World as Lover, World as Self,* we have some companion wisdom for the long journey. Macy's teachings over the past 30 years have been foundational for many activists and citizens anxious about the deteriorating state of the planet. Year after year, the concerns have mounted—from pesticides to groundwater pollution, from factory farms to rainforest destruction. At times and in places, it has seemed the earth could not withstand the degree of assault inflicted upon it by its human inhabitants. Joanna Macy has offered visionary yet pragmatic leadership in facing the emotional pain of this assault. Her workshops around the world have galvanized thousands of people to take action. Using the powerful frameworks of systems analysis and ecopsychology, Macy provides tools that are effective in even the most daunting situations.

But more than tools, these chapters are filled with gifts of the heart and mind. Macy presents a way to be with seemingly impossible challenges, drawing on ancient teachings of the Buddha as well as modern views of eco-social systems. Here we find the core work of her doctoral research, more relevant than ever to environmental work today. She urges us to "come home again" to the world as both self and lover, to feel the way we are actually all connected—not in some fuzzy mystical trance state but in the very real material exchanges of air, water, flesh, and heat. Macy invites us to experience the ecological self, the way each of us is an expression of much larger self-organizing patterns.

As the decades have advanced, and environmental concerns seem only to multiply, many people shrug their shoulders and give up, convinced they cannot stop the bulldozer of progress. Joanna Macy takes the long view, investing in what she calls The Third Turning. Gazing into the future she sees the shift to Life-Sustaining Society already taking place, being called forth by ordinary citizens. For her the Great Work of this time is a fabulous adventure, risky on every front, but completely worth the effort. In these pages you can almost hear her spunky laughter ring out. How could we not join her on this great journey toward sanity and health?

It can be all too tempting to fall into the trap of feeling sorry for ourselves. How did we ever get into this overwhelmingly complex fix? Macy wastes no time in blame or anger, but takes the path of gratitude and grace. For her it is a grand privilege to be alive at this time, working together for this beautiful earth that has given us life. I see her now with that bright look in her eyes, gazing into the distance, hearing the prophecy of the Shambhala warrior. For Macy this is no dream, it is a potent human reality, limited only by our own small imaginations. This vision of a sustainable future will require, as she says, a "burning patience" and a willingness to be completely present to the larger whole.

It is a personal honor to introduce this new edition of Joanna's work. For me, like many others, Joanna has been an inspiration, a guide, and a friend along the way. Her wisdom and rich imagination have brought life-giving energy to environmentally concerned citizens around the world. We are fortunate indeed to have such an articulate and impassioned teacher in these demanding times. It is my abiding hope that we can continue to keep each other company as each of us takes up the next piece of the "work that reconnects."

—Stephanie Kaza

INTRODUCTION

THE ADVENTURES flowing into this book differ greatly in circumstance. Some happened while exploring ancient texts, others while preparing testimony on nuclear waste disposal. Some arose while translating Rainer Maria Rilke's poetry or riding to the ruins of a Tibetan monastery. Yet they all reflect the same concern.

Carl Jung said that at the core of each life's journey is one question we are born to pursue. The one question threading through my life here on this beautiful Earth is about how to be fully present to my world—present enough to rejoice and be useful—while we as a species are progressively destroying it. This book is my attempt to answer this preoccupation, as well as insight into the relief and guidance I have found in the teachings of the Buddha.

Since each chapter is shaped as a response to the same question, the chapters don't need to be read in sequence. Yet I like the order in which they appear. It mirrors my growing fascination with the play of time, and the fruitful presence in our lives of ancestors and future generations.

Part One casts an appreciative eye on the past. In what ways can our forebears help us to see our current world without fear and self-loathing? The title chapter delineates the four age-old ways we humans have seen our world: as a battlefield, as a trap, as a lover, and even as our larger self. The last two are rooted in appreciation of our profound interconnectedness with all that is. The following chapters turn to the Buddha's central teaching, the interdependence of all things, and what that can mean for us now. They draw substantially on my book *Mutual Causality in Buddhism and General Systems Theory.** I close this section with the love of my life—at least the numinous, nonphysical part of it—which is the Mother of All Buddhas. This feminine archetype of wisdom is for me an intellectual delight, emotional ground, and inner authority.

Part Two details the ways our ancestors' wisdom is embodied in our lives today. Here I draw from my trainings for activists in the Work That Reconnects, an evolving body of group practices based on systems theory, deep ecology, and Buddhist teachings, and that is described in my book *Coming Back to Life.*** This section begins with gratitude, whose constant and true power can carry us in this dark time. It strengthens us to go into the grief we carry on behalf of the world and its beings, ourselves included. There, we discover our mutual belonging. Ancestral voices are heard again in the Shambhala Warrior prophecy, coming through with special relevance to this moment on Earth. Before closing this section, I share specific spiritual practices that can help us take heart.

Part Three invites us to see our lives from the perspective of future generations. Awareness of our deep connection with those who come after lifts our hearts and keeps us going. This section also elaborates on the Great Turning, the revolutionary transition we need to make from the industrial growth society to a life-sustaining society. Basic to this revolution is the arising of an ecological identity, "the greening of the self," as well as a readiness to persevere for the long haul. The book comes to completion with chapters conveying more explicitly the inspiration that we can receive from future generations. Ancient Buddhist scriptures weigh in again, attesting to the dependent coarising of past, present, and future. And equally welcome are the

* *Mutual Causality in Buddhism and General Systems Theory* by Joanna Macy (Albany, NY: SUNY Press, 1991).
** *Coming Back to Life* by Joanna Macy (Gabriola Island, B.C., Canada: New Society Publishers, 1998).

practical steps we can take now to protect irreplaceable strands of our natural world.

I am grateful to Parallax Press for inviting me to prepare the revised edition of this book. I didn't know how big a job it would turn out to be—going over every page with a fine-toothed comb, culling, reshaping, and adding so it can reflect what has happened to my world and to me in the last sixteen years. It's a blessing because the learning that I harvested through each of these adventures of heart and mind well up for me now with fresh significance, deepening my gladness for being alive. They confirm the privilege of being on hand in this historical moment, when a quantum leap of consciousness is required if complex life forms are to survive on Earth.

And I want to express gratitude to the people who helped make this book possible. First of all, there is Arnie Kotler, founder of Parallax Press. After hearing me talk on this subject, he drove me home and strongly encouraged me to make a book about it. Swiftly, he helped me put it together and saw it into print. Sixteen years later Rachel Neumann, Senior Editor at Parallax, called to say that it was time for a revised edition. I am thankful for that, as well as for her insightful care in seeing it through, and the format she proposed. Since the revision involved a lot more effort than I anticipated, I am enduringly grateful for Aryeh Shell. With her wits, skill, and knowledge of my work, she helped me create this book in a vibrant fashion. Finally, in deepest homage, I bow to all my teachers and to the Buddhadharma, for the wonder of life they have helped me to see.

PART ONE:

Harvesting Wisdom from the Past

World as Lover, World as Self   I

Another world is not only possible, she is on her way.
On a quiet day, I can hear her breathing.
—ARUNDHATI ROY

L IFE ON OUR PLANET is in trouble. It is hard to go anywhere without being confronted by the wounding of our world, the tearing
of the very fabric of life. We are assaulted by news of tor-
nadoes and hurricanes, fleeing refugees, an entire village buried in
mudslides, thousands of bodies under the rubble, another species lost,
another city bombed.

Our planet is sending us signals of distress that are so continual
now they seem almost normal. Reports proliferate about the loss of
cropland and the spreading of hunger, toxins in the air we breathe and
the water we drink, the die-off of plant and animal species. These are
warning signals that we live in a world that can end, at least as a home
for conscious life. This is not to say that it *will* end, but it *can* end. That
very possibility changes everything for us.

There have been small groups throughout history that have pro-
claimed the end of the world, such as at the time of the first millen-
nium and again during the Black Plague in Europe. These expectations
arose within the context of religious faith, of a belief in a just but angry
God ready to punish his wayward children. But now the prospect is
spelled out in sober scientific data, not religious belief, and it is entirely
devoid of transcendent meaning. I stress the unprecedented nature of

our situation, because I want to inspire respect and compassion for what we are experiencing.

With isolated exceptions, every generation prior to ours lived with the assumption that other generations would follow. It has been an integral part of the human experience to take it for granted that the work of our hands and heads and hearts could live on through those who came after us, walking the same Earth, beneath the same sky. Plagues, wars, and personal death have always taken place within that wider context, the assurance of continuity. Now we have lost the certainty that there will be a future for humans. I believe that this loss, felt at some level of consciousness by everyone, regardless of political orientation, is the pivotal psychological reality of our time.

Internal and external forces are at work urging us to look away from the reality of what is happening. Television, iPods, cell phones, and all the newest electronic games and gadgets engulf us with distractions and mind-numbing entertainment. The use of antidepressants, substance abuse, and suicide rates, especially among young people, are dramatically on the rise. The World Health Organization reports that depression has reached epidemic proportions and is predicted to be the second leading cause of death by 2020.* Nearly four million people across the globe have plugged into Second Life, a virtual world in which to live and buy property far from the global crises of our fractured Earth. Many of us seem to be doing everything we can to shut off awareness of the real world's plight.

To others of us, the distress of people and planet brings a near-desperate sense of urgency to do something. But the many programs, strategies, and causes that vie for our attention, also bring a sense of overwhelm. It is hard to know which of the countless separate issues we should address first; and our confusion makes it hard to see their linkages and common roots.

---

* http://www.who.int/mental_health/management/depression/definition/en
http://www.who.int/mental_health/prevention/suicide/suicideprevent/en

In the face of what is happening, how do we avoid feeling overwhelmed and just giving up? Instead of turning to the diversions and demands of our consumer society, how can we stay alert to what's really going on?

Among the inner resources that help us connect with the events of our time is what Germans call *weltbild,* the way we picture our world and relate to it. By looking at our weltbild, we can discover ways that best steady and embolden us to do what must be done.

There are four ways of looking at the world that have been passed down to us through the ages. They are not specific to any culture or tradition. You can find all of them in all the major religions. These four are: world as battlefield, world as trap, world as lover, and world as self.

World as Battlefield

Many people view the world as battleground where good and evil are pitted against each other and forces of light struggle against the forces of darkness. This way of seeing, reinforced by millennia of living with war, can be traced back to the ancient Zoroastrians and Manichaeans. It can be persuasive, especially when we feel threatened. Such a view is very good for arousing courage, summoning up the blood, using the fiery energies of anger and militancy.

It is very good, too, for lending a sense of certainty. Whatever the score may be at the moment or whatever the tactics you're employing, there is the reassuring sense that you are fighting God's battle—and that ultimately you will win. William Irwin Thompson has called this kind of certainty and the self-righteousness that goes with it, the "apartheid of good."

It is a powerful force in many areas of our world today, from the Middle East to the Philippines, and it has taken hold in the United States with the War on Terror and the president's assertion that "you're either with us or against us." When he proclaims the existence of an "axis of evil," the whole world becomes a battleground. Thus,

U.S. military expenditures soar, accounting for half of the world's total.

It's not just politicians who fall prey to the battlefield frame of mind. To be constantly fighting the bad guys, be they corporations or riot police, can bring citizens and grassroots activists to the point of exhaustion and hopelessness. A do-or-die militancy, combined with some self-righteousness, is a recipe for burnout, or at the very least a loss of resilience and creativity.

There are those who tell us we can join a divinely ordained battle, leading to Armageddon and the Second Coming of Christ. In this variety of Christian thought, nuclear war may be the catalyst for the millennial denouement, bringing rewards to the elect who will inherit the Earth—and the bomb itself can appear as an instrument of God's will. Their interpretation of biblical revelation has become a force in American politics, from foreign to environmental policy.

A more innocuous version of the battlefield image of the world is the one I learned from my grandparents. It is the world as a classroom, or a kind of moral gymnasium, where you are put through tests to prove your mettle and shape you up, so that you can graduate to other arenas and rewards. Whether imagined as a school or battlefield, the world is a proving ground, with little worth other than that. Our immortal souls are being tested here. They count, and the world doesn't. Indeed, in today's battles for dominance or survival, the world counts for so little that it's being destroyed.

This point of view is contagious. It spreads rapidly through fear-inducing propaganda. It is aggravated by violent video games that train minds to engage in the virtual destruction of the "other." It is taught and celebrated in our schools through war-dominated historical narratives. The spread of poverty and desperation throughout the globe generates new waves of fundamentalism. The world as battlefield can be seen on every corner, in every newspaper, on every news channel. We cannot break out of this destructive paradigm without first recognizing its presence, appeal, and tenacity.

World as Trap

The second view is the world as trap. In this view, the goal is not to engage in struggle and vanquish the foe, but to disentangle ourselves and escape from this messy world. We try to extricate ourselves and ascend to a higher, supra-phenomenal plane. This stance is based on the view of reality where mind is seen as higher than nature, and spirit is set over and above the flesh. This view encourages contempt for the material plane. It has entered the major religions of the last 5,000 years, regardless of their metaphysics.

Many of us on spiritual paths fall for this perspective. Wanting to affirm a transcendent reality distinct from a materialistic society, we place it on a supra-phenomenal level removed from confusion and suffering. We assign the tranquility found in spiritual practices to a haven that is aloof from our world and to which we can ascend and be safe and serene. This gets tricky, because we still have bodies and are dependent on them, however advanced we may be on the spiritual path.

Trying to escape from something that we are dependent on breeds a love-hate relationship. This love-hate relationship with matter permeates our culture and breeds a deep ambivalence. We want to both possess and destroy. These two impulses, craving and aversion, inflame each other in a vicious circle. We can see this exemplified in my country's skyrocketing military buildup. To back up our demands for the raw materials, we threaten our very existence. To sustain our technologies' capacity to destroy, we require increasing amounts of raw materials; and the vicious circle intensifies.

A love-hate relationship with matter reinforces the idea that mind and spirit are separate from the natural world, and superior to it. Dichotomies arise between spirit and flesh, light and dark, reason and emotion, male and female, sacred and secular. The desire to possess or destroy becomes easily projected onto the Earth, the female, dark emotions, and dark-skinned people. It feeds into the dominant model of power-over and societal systems of oppression. We can see our centuries of racism, colonialism, imperialism, exploitation, and the raping of earth and women as tragic consequences of the notion that the world is a trap.

Many on a spiritual path, seeking to transcend all impulses to acquire or to destroy, put great value on detachment. They are reluctant to engage in the hurly-burly work of social change. They often avoid looking at the ways in which they themselves benefit from systems that perpetuate oppression.

Some Buddhists seem to understand detachment as freedom from the world and indifference to its fate. But the Buddha taught detachment from ego, not detachment from the world. In fact, the Buddha was suspicious of those who tried to detach themselves from the material realm. Referring to yogis who mortified the flesh in order to free the spirit, the Buddha likened their efforts to those of a dog tied by a rope to a stake in the ground. He said that the harder they tried to free themselves from the body, the more they would circle round and get closer to the stake, eventually wrapping themselves around it.

Of course, even when you see the world as a trap, you can still feel a compassionate impulse to help its suffering beings. In that case, the personal and the political are often viewed in a sequential fashion. "I'll find peace within myself first, then I'll join actions to stop the war." Those who are not engaged in spiritual pursuits put it differently: "I'll get my head straight first—I'll get psychoanalyzed, I'll overcome my inhibitions or neuroses or hang-ups—and *then* I'll wade into the fray." Presupposing that world and self are essentially separate, they imagine they can heal one before healing the other. This stance conveys the impression that human consciousness inhabits some haven, or locker room, independent of the collective situation—and then trots onto the playing field when it is geared up and ready.

Another hazard of this view is fear of nature, especially during these uncertain times of immense climate change. The increasing devastation wrought by storms and unpredictable weather patterns is perceived by some as the wrath of our Mother Earth. Even environmentalists can portray nature as an object of fear and loathing, as in the title of James Lovelock's book on global warming, *The Revenge of Gaia*. But if we are an inseparable part of the natural world, who is the world taking revenge upon, itself? Such a stance obscures our deepest connections, and isolates us from the source of our greatest wisdom.

It is my experience that the world itself has a role to play in our spiritual liberation. Its very pressures, pains, and risks can wake us up—release us from the bonds of ego and guide us home to our vast, true nature.

World as Lover

In this third view, the world is experienced not as a stage set for our moral battles or a prison to escape from, but an essential and life-giving partner. From the curve of the cosmos to the spinning of atoms, the universe engages in a dance of mutual allurement.

Hindu culture has many expressions of our erotic relationship to the world. In early Vedic hymns, the first stirrings of life are equated with the primal pulse of eros. In the beginning there was the sacred self-existent one, Prajapati. Lonely, it created the world by splitting into two so that it could copulate with itself. Pregnant with its own inner amplitude and tension, out of desire it gave birth to all phenomena.

In this worldview, desire plays a creative, world-manifesting role. Its charge in Hinduism pulses onward into Krishna worship, where devotional songs, or *bhajan*s, draw on the yearnings of body and soul. Krishna evokes these yearnings in his devotees to bring them to the bliss of union with the divine. As you sing your longing for the dewdrop sparkle of his eyes, the nectar of his lips, the blue shade of his skin, like the thunderclouds that bring the refreshment and fertility of the monsoon, the whole world takes on his beauty and the sweetness of his flesh. You feel yourself embraced in the primal play of life.

As the thirteenth century Hindu poet, Jnaneshwar, sang in his "Nectar of Self-Awareness," this ecstatic play is ever-present in each single manifestation of life.

The lover, out of boundless love
takes the form of the Beloved.
What Beauty!
Both are made of the same nectar
and share the same food.

Out of the Supreme Love
they swallow each other up.
But separate again for the joy of being two. . . .

The entire universe
is too small to contain them.
Yet they live happily
in the tiniest particle.

That erotic affirmation of the phenomenal world is not limited to Hinduism. Ancient Goddess religions carry it too, as do strains of Sufism and the Kabbalah. Even Christianity has its tradition of bridal mysticism.

This view of world as lover also occurs outside of religious metaphor. A poet friend of mine, left by her partner, was catapulted into extreme grief and loneliness. Leaving her rural community, she moved to New York City, took a single bare room, and walked the city streets for months. Through walking, she eventually found her wholeness again. She said, "I learned to move in the world as if it were my lover."

In his little book, *Cosmicomics,* Italian storyteller Italo Calvino describes the evolution of life from the perspective of an individual who experienced it from the beginning. One chapter begins with a scientific statement: "Through the calculations begun by Edwin P. Hubble on the galaxies' velocity of recession, we can establish the moment when all the universe's matter was concentrated in a single point, before it began to expand in space."

"We were all there, where else could we have been?" says Calvino's narrator, Qfwfq. He then goes on to describe his experience:

We were all in that one point—and, man, was it crowded! Contrary to what you might think, it wasn't the sort of situation that encourages sociability. . . . Given the conditions, irritations were almost inevitable. See, in addition to all those people, you have to add all the stuff we had to keep piled up in there: all the material that was to serve afterwards to form the universe . . . from the nebula of Andromeda to the Vosges Mountains to beryllium isotopes. And on top of that we were always bumping against the Z'zu family's household goods: camp beds, mattresses, baskets. . . .

So there were, naturally enough, complaints and gossip, but none ever attached to Signora Pavacini. (Since most names in the story have no vowels, I have given her a name we can pronounce.) "Signora Pavacini, her bosom, her thighs, her orange dressing gown," the sheer memory of her fills our narrator:

with a blissful, generous emotion . . . the fact that she went to bed with her friend Mr. DeXueaux was well known. But in a point, if there's a bed, it takes up the whole point, so it isn't a question of *going* to bed but of *being* there, because anybody in the point is also in the bed. So consequently it was inevitable that she was in bed with each of us. If she'd been another person, there's no telling all the things that might have been said about her. . . .

This state of affairs could have gone on indefinitely, but something extraordinary happened. An idea occurred to Signora Pavacini: "Oh boys, if only I had some room, how I'd like to make some pasta for you!" Here I quote in part from my favorite longest sentence in literature, which closes this particular chapter in Calvino's collection:

And in that moment we all thought of the space that her round arms would occupy moving backward and forward over the great mound of flour and eggs . . . while her arms kneaded and kneaded, white and shiny with oil up to the elbows, and we thought of the space the flour would occupy and the wheat for the flour and the fields to raise the wheat and the mountains from which the water would flow to irrigate the fields . . . of the space it would take for the Sun to arrive with its rays, to ripen the wheat; of the space for the Sun to condense from the clouds of stellar gases and burn; of the quantities of stars and galaxies and galactic masses in flight through space which would be needed to hold suspended every galaxy, every nebula, every sun, every planet, and at the same time we thought of it, this space was inevitably being formed, at the same time that Mrs. Pavacini was uttering those words: ". . . ah, what pasta, boys!" the point that contained her and all of us was expanding in a halo of distance in light years and light centuries and billions of light millennia and we were being hurled to the four corners of the universe . . . and she dissolved into I don't know what kind of energy-light-heat, she, Signora Pavacini, she who in the midst of our closed, petty world had been capable of a generous impulse, "Boys, the pasta I could make for you!" a true outburst of general love, initiating at the same time the concept of space and, properly speaking, space itself, and time, and universal gravitation, and the gravitating universe, making possible billions and billions of suns, and planets, and fields of wheat, and Signoras Pavacinis scattered through the continents of the planets, kneading with floury, oil-shiny, generous arms, and she lost at that very moment, and we, mourning her loss.

But is she lost? Or is she equally present, in every moment, her act of love embodied in every unfolding of this amazing world? Whether we see it as Krishna or as Signora Pavacini, that teasing, loving presence is in the monsoon clouds and the peacock's cry that heralds monsoon, and in the plate of good pasta. For when you see the world as lover, every being can become—if you have a clever, appreciative eye—an expression of that ongoing, erotic impulse. It takes form right now in each one of us and in everyone and everything we encounter—the bus driver, the cop at the corner, the leaping squirrel. As we seek to discover the lover in each life form, we can find ourselves in the dance of *rasa-lila*, sweet play, where each of the milkmaids who yearned for Krishna finds him magically at her side, her very own partner in the dance. The one beloved becomes many, and the world itself is her lover.

World as Self

Just as lovers seek union, we are apt, when we fall in love with our world, to fall into oneness with it as well. We begin to see the world as ourselves. Hunger for this union springs from a deep knowing, which mystics of all traditions give voice to. Breaking open a seed to reveal its life-giving kernel, the sage in the Upanishads tells his student: "*Tat tvam asi*—That art thou." The tree that will grow from the seed, that art thou; the running water, that art thou; and the sun in the sky, and all that is, that art thou.

"There is a Secret One inside us," says Kabir, "the planets in all the galaxies pass through his hands like beads." Mystics of the Abrahamic religions speak of merging self with God rather than with the world, but the import is often the same. When Hildegard of Bingen experienced unity with the divine, she gave it these words: "I am the breeze that nurtures all things green . . . I am the rain coming from the dew that causes the grasses to laugh with the joy of life."

Indigenous traditions around the globe know the self as one with its world. Nature is alive and seamlessly whole, often symbolized by a circle: the sacred hoop of life. Not only our fate, but also our identity is interwoven with all beings. Native American writer-poet Scott Momaday sings it this way:

I am a feather on the bright sky.
I am the blue horse that runs on the plain.
I am the fish that rolls, shining, in the water,
I am the shadow that follows a child . . .
I am the hunger of a young wolf.
I am the whole dream of things.
You see, I am alive, I am alive.

The fifteenth century cardinal Nicholas of Cusa defined God as an infinite circle whose periphery is nowhere and whose center is everywhere. That center, that one self, is in you and me and the tree outside the door. Similarly, the Jeweled Net of Indra, the vision of reality that arose with Hua Yen Buddhism, reveals a world where each being, each gem at each node of the net, is illumined by all the others and reflected in them. As part of this world, you contain the whole of it.

We don't have to surrender our individuality to experience the world as an extended self and its story as our own extended story. The liver, leg, and lung that are "mine" are highly distinct from each other, thank goodness, and each has a distinctive role to play. The larger "selfness" we discover today is not an undifferentiated unity. As in all living systems, intelligence depends on the integrative play of diversity. Diversity is a source of resilience. This is good news because this time of great challenge demands more commitment, endurance, and courage than any one of us can dredge up out of our own individual supply. We can learn to draw on the other neurons in the neural net and view them with gratitude. The acts and intentions of others are like seeds that can germinate and bear fruit through our own lives, as we take them in and dedicate that awareness to the healing of our world.

Now it can dawn on us: we are our world knowing itself. We can relinquish our isolation. We can come home again to a world that can appear to us now both as self and as lover. Relating to our world with the full measure of our being, we partake of the qualities of both. In his poem, "The Old Mendicant," Vietnamese Zen Master Thich

Nhat Hanh evokes the long, wondrous evolutionary journey we all have made together, from which we are as inseparable as from our own selves. At the same time, it is a love song. Hear these lines, as if addressed to you:

> Being rock, being gas, being mist, being Mind,
> being the mesons traveling among galaxies at the speed of light,
> you have come here, my beloved. . . .
> You have manifested yourself
> as trees, grass, butterflies, single-celled beings,
> and as chrysanthemums.
> But the eyes with which you looked at me this morning
> tell me you have never died.

We have all gone on that long journey, and now, richer for it, we come home to our mutual belonging. We return to the experience that we are both the self of our world and its cherished lover. We are not doomed to destroy it by the cravings of the separate ego and the technologies it fashioned. We can wake up to who we really are, allow the rivers to flow clean once more, and the trees to grow green along their banks.

IT'S ALL CONNECTED

2

It's All Alive. It's All Intelligent. It's All Connected.
—BIONEERS CONFERENCE MOTTO

T HESE WORDS HAVE AN ancestral ring. They echo something we've heard from time immemorial. Revived and repeated in our world today, references to our interconnectedness have become so commonplace they can seem to be little more than a harmless truism.

The familiarity of these words obscures the life-changing implications that emerge if we take them seriously. Then they are like a startling message, slapping us awake. For to truly perceive all life as interconnected challenges many of our most automatic assumptions about what we are and what we need. It can lead us to see the world not as a battlefield or a trap, but as a wellspring of our body and mind, and so intrinsic to our well-being that it can be more aptly viewed as lover or larger self.

For our daily pursuits and frame of mind, what does it mean to be a living part of a living whole, like a cell in the body of Earth? Such a question, when we pursue it, brings us back to ancestral wisdom. To harvest this kind of wisdom, let's turn to the Buddha's teachings, known as the Dharma; for in no other body of thought has the interdependence of all things played so specific and central a role. And none other has influenced more deeply my own life and work.

Dependent Co-arising

The Buddha called our interconnectedness *paticca samuppada,* dependent co-arising. It is equated with the Dharma in both meanings of that term: the Buddha's teachings and the law of life itself. "They who see paticca samuppada see the Dharma," said the Buddha, "and they who see the Dharma see paticca samuppada."

This centerpiece of the Buddha's teaching is not about a dimension of reality separate from our daily lives. It refers to no absolute or eternal essence, but to the way things work, how events happen and relate to each other. Perceiving all existence as a dynamic, self-sustaining web of relations, it stood in stark contrast to the other schools of thought circulating in India of the sixth century.

Gautama Siddhartha, the man who became the Buddha, left a life of luxury and privilege to seek liberating wisdom. He engaged in years of advanced yogic practices under the most highly reputed masters of his time. But he found no teachings capable of explaining and resolving the canker at the core of human experience: how we create suffering for ourselves and for others. So then, relying on his own unswerving determination, he finally stopped wandering and sat under a shady tree, committing himself to stay there until he reached some insight into this mystery.

Sitting under the tree, he began not with abstractions or religious beliefs, but with his own experience, focusing on the immediate existential aspects of life. He traced how the basic factors of being alive, such as awareness, sensation, feeling, wanting, give rise to each other.

In so doing, he found no first cause or prime mover. Instead he beheld patterns and circuits of contingency, arising and sustained by their own interplay. It was then, in the crucible of his unwavering attention, that the realization of dependent co-arising swept upon him.

The Mahapadana Sutta says:

> Coming to be, coming to be! . . . Ceasing to be, ceasing to be! At that thought, brethren, there arose . . . a vision of

things not before called to mind, and knowledge arose. . . .
Such is form, such is the coming to be of form, such is its
passing away. . . . Such is cognition, such is its coming to be,
such is its passing away. And [he abided] in the discernment
of the arising and passing away.

The process nature of reality became clear. He beheld the flowing
interaction of all things as they provide occasion and context for each
other's emergence and subsiding—each as real as the air we breathe,
each as transient as the gestures of a dance.

All aspects of our world and all factors of our lives subsist, he saw,
in a dynamic web of interdependence. But those currents of relationship are not visible. To the physical eye we look like separate projects
walking around in separate bodies. And, as such, we vie with each
other for a place in the sun and compete for resources to meet our
own private needs and desires. With such a lens on life, we feel we
must protect ourselves by building tall fences, gated communities, and
militarized borders.

Still, the fact of our interdependence suggests that we are capable of
seeing and interacting in more harmonious ways, like living parts of a
single living whole. Arising out of the web of life, our mutual belonging is not a vain and sentimental dream.

The Buddha knew that the understanding that had come upon him
would be difficult to convey, for it goes against the grain of both
our sensory experience and our desire for security. So, when he arose
from his enlightenment vigil, he was tempted not to teach.

The Mahapadana Sutta continues:

I have penetrated this truth, deep, hard to perceive, hard
to understand, calm, sublime, beyond logic, subtle, intel-
ligible only to the wise. But this is a race devoting itself to
the things to which it clings. . . . And for such a race this
were a matter hard to perceive, to wit, that all co-arises
interdependently.

The mission at first seemed too daunting to undertake. According to the legend it was the god Brahma who reminded him: "There are those perishing from not hearing the truth; they will come to be knowers of the truth. . . . There are those who will understand." Thereupon, out of compassion, the Buddha set forth to teach. One of the earliest formulations of the central teaching was a four-part statement:

> This being, that becomes.
> From the arising of this, that arises.
> This not being, that becomes not.
> From the ceasing of this, that ceases.

According to this deceptively simple set of assertions, things do not produce each other or make each other happen, as in linear causality. They *help* each other happen by providing occasion or locus or context, and in so doing, they in turn are affected. There is a reciprocal dynamic at play. Power inheres not in any one dominating entity, but in the relationship between entities.

From our dependent co-arising, the Four Noble Truths emerged. In their traditional and highly condensed form, these are the truth of suffering (*dukkha*), the truth about our suffering's cause (*samudaya*), the truth of its cessation (*nirodha*), and the path (*magga*) leading to its cessation. As they are elaborated throughout the Buddha's teachings, their meanings become richly relevant to our lives.

The First Noble Truth invites us to acknowledge the suffering we cause ourselves and each other, and the frustrations endemic to our lives. With the Second, we recognize that we create our own bondage, as we try to grasp and identify with what is essentially impermanent. The Third Noble Truth would have us realize that suffering, arising in this fashion, is not inevitable; it can cease as we learn to see and honor the interdependence of all things. With the Fourth, we determine to walk the path that embodies this learning, and cleanse our perceptions through meditation and moral conduct.

The teaching of paticca samuppada struck Ananda, the Buddha's faithful attendant, with awe and enthusiasm. "Wonderful, Lord, marvelous, Lord, is the depth of this causal law and deep it appears," he said. "And yet I reckon it as ever so plain."

"Say not so, Ananda, say not so!" replied the Buddha. "Deep indeed is this causal law, and deep indeed it appears. It is through not knowing, not penetrating that doctrine, that this generation has become entangled like a ball of string and covered with blight, unable to pass over the doom of the waste, the woeful way, the constant faring on."

The Buddha could say the same thing to our current generation as we continue to get stuck in our ways of perceiving and knowing, separating self from that which it observes, distancing mind from body.

The Co-arising of Knower and Known

One sunny morning on a street corner in Berkeley, I ran into a woman I had met at a meditation retreat. We stopped to talk, calling each other's attention to the beauty of the day. When she asked, "How are you doing?" I lifted the newspaper in my hand, with its headlines about increasing body counts in the Middle East. "I'm worried sick that we are creating an endless war."

Ella listened for a moment, then shook her head in sweet concern and smiled. "Those are just passing events," she said. "If you focus on them like that you just add to the suffering. From a higher perspective, it is all in our minds." She went on to tell me how we "create our own reality" and how I should see through the material world to the realm of pure spirit.

I started to protest that the events troubling me were as real as the sun on the sidewalk. I wanted to say, "Tell that to the Iraqi children we're bombing!" I didn't want my anguish over my country's war-making trivialized. Later, when I stopped seething, I realized that we had been taking part in a very ancient conversation. What is real? Is reality out there, in the world I behold, or is it inside, just in my mind?

The mystery of the relation between mind, which we subjectively experience, and the world outside it, which we objectively perceive, has teased humankind since we first reflected on the nature of things. Walking the Earth with a battery of senses, we see, hear, taste, touch, and smell it—we feel we know the contours and colors of our world, its texture and topography. Yet, at the same time, it can seem as if we live more truly in the inner realm where we receive these impressions and reflect upon them.

Is it all just as I perceive it? Or am I making it up? These eternal questions bemuse the mind of the growing child. Among philosophers they engender the pursuit of epistemology, the study of how we know things.

In debating the relative reality of perceiver and perceived, mainstream Western thought has tended to stress exclusively one or the other. Classical empiricists hold that the world is the cause of our perceptions: unquestionably there, it registers its data on passive and neutral sense organs. These data are taken as "given," as Thomas Kuhn observes: "Is sensory data fixed and neutral? Are theories simply given data? The epistemological viewpoint that has most often guided Western philosophy dictates an immediate and unequivocal yes."

But of course there are those thinkers and traditions that have disagreed. Fascinated by the power of the mind, subjective idealists view external phenomena as projections of the mind. Consciousness is primary and independent of the impressions it receives.

These two positions, still vying for allegiance in our day, were vigorously debated in ancient India during the Buddha's life. Instead of taking sides, Gautama opened a third alternative. He taught that knower and known, mind and world, arise interdependently.

This teaching is important for us to grasp, as we free ourselves from the reductionism of classical science, where only external phenomena are seen as really real. Without it we can easily flip over into the opposite and equally one-sided extreme. Like Ella in Berkeley, we can imagine that the world we see is only a projection of our minds and that we create it unilaterally.

Returning for a moment to early India, it's worth noting that the

Buddha took pains to distinguish his teachings from those of the Upa-nishads. There, all perception and knowing are the function of the Atman, an eternal, universal Self at the core of one's being. "There is no other seer than he, no other hearer than he. . . . " The Atman is the silent witness, the imperturbable rider of the chariot, spectator of all events.

In contrast, the Buddha taught that perceiving and knowing hap-pen through a convergence of factors, namely a sense organ, a sense object, and the contact between them. Knowing is transactional. Like a fire that cannot burn without the wood or dried grass on which it feeds, all consciousness requires an object.

Because he did not see it as existing prior to or independently of the world it knows, the Buddha rejected *a priori* reasoning. He posited no realm of pure logic aloof from the sensory world.

> Were a man to say: I shall show the coming, the going, the passing away, the arising, the growth, the increase or devel-opment of consciousness apart from body, sensation, per-ception, and volitional formations, he would be speaking about something which does not exist.

The "volitional formations," called *sankhara* in the original Pali, are the habits and tendencies generated by previous activity. They load our sense impressions and cognitions with the freight of past experi-ences and associations. We see the world through filters upon filters of time, culture, race, class, gender, and a host of other subjective and social identities.

Perception, then, is a highly interpretive process. We create our worlds, but we do not do so unilaterally, for consciousness is colored by that upon which it feeds; subject and object are interdependent. The Buddha denied neither the "thereness" of the sense objects nor the projective capacities of the mind; he simply saw the process as a two-way street.

If that is the case, any pursuit of final certainty or claim to an absolute truth is doomed. For all knowing is relative to the perspective of the knower and conditioned by his past experience.

Gautama was unique among teachers of his time in refusing to make definitive statements on metaphysical matters. To the exasperation of many of his followers, he refused to speculate on topics that are not accessible to direct, personal experience, such as the existence of a creator or the reality of an afterlife. Assertions on such matters, he said, are necessarily partial, and become objects of attachment. He dismissed them with barely disguised contempt.

The Buddha said:

> Whatever is esteemed as truth by other folk, amidst those who are entrenched in their own views . . . I hold none as true or false. This barb I beheld well in advance, whereon mankind is impaled: "I know, I see, 'tis verily so"—no such clinging for the Tathagatas.

I love this sly and pithy observation. He does not say they are wrong who assert, "I know, I see, 'tis verily so." He just says that they are hooked, that they are not free. And he is glad not to be hooked himself—"no such clinging for the Tathagatas" (another word for Buddhas).

The quote reminds me of Dr. A. T. Ariyaratne, founder of Sarvodaya, the Buddhist-inspired community development movement in Sri Lanka. One day I accompanied Ari, as he is called by his friends, on a visit to a Sarvodaya rural center, and we ran across a Western guru in robes who preached to us the whole time, serenely oozing his certitude of ultimate truth. When Ari and I got back in the car, I vented my irritation at the pompous fellow, pointing out emphatically how wrong he was. Ari just laughed and said, "Looks like he's 'impaled on the barb.' But you don't need to be!"

The impossibility of arriving at ultimate formulations of reality does not represent a defeat for the inquiring mind. So long as we claim no authority beyond our own experience, what we speak has the ring of truth.

Co-arising of Body and Mind

The processes of the mind are so pervasive that they can seem more real to us than anything else. Our thoughts can easily be taken as more worthy and reliable than the material realm in which we are embedded. When this happens, as it does in most religious traditions of the patriarchal era, a split occurs, separating us from the natural world and the wisdom of our own bodies. The Buddha warned us against this, and took pains to illuminate the radical interdependence of mind and matter.

This is important because the environmental crisis has deep attitudinal roots. The bulldozing of nature and the abuse of our own bodies reveal the split in the psyche that cuts us off from the physical world. This separation engenders a fear of nature and a compulsion to control it. To fill the emptiness caused by this perceived separation, we seek satisfaction with external diversions, be it alcohol, tobacco, crack, or shopping.

What ways of thinking can help us come home again to the physical world? Marxism, capitalism, and classical science offer little help. Their materialism does not heal the separation, because they give no authority to subjective experience.

When we turn instead to spirituality, we find that the major religious traditions of patriarchal culture are afflicted with the same split—a deadening dichotomy between matter and mind. Behind their theologies and symbol systems, we detect a revulsion toward the flesh. As I became acquainted with Buddhism and experienced the luminous beauty of its teachings about the mind, I began to wonder what the Dharma had to say about the body. Did it accord reality and dignity to the physical? Was it free of contempt for matter?

In ancient India, too, there were contending schools of thought as to the relation of mind and body. The materialists reduced mind to matter, and the Vedantans reduced matter to mind. The Buddha, taking a different approach, did not explain one in terms of the other, nor question the reality of either. Instead he showed how they co-arise in interaction. Here is an early image he and his followers used to convey the relation of mind to body:

> Two sheaves of reeds leaning one against the other. Even so, friend, name-and-form comes to pass conditioned by con-sciousness, consciousness conditioned by name-and-form .... If, friend, I were to pull towards me one of those sheaves of reeds, the other would fall; if I were to pull towards me the other, the former would fall.

This teaching can be puzzling to those of us familiar with ascetic passages in the early scriptures, and the practices they enjoin for cultivating disdain of the body. It is true that monks were urged to contemplate the body in terms of "kidneys, liver, spleen, intestines, feces, phlegm, pus, mucus, urine. . . . " Yet the body was not dismissed as less real or less valuable than consciousness, reason, or intellect. As the monk was to meditate on the impermanent and composite nature of the body, so was he also to meditate on the composite and transient nature of the mind.

Mind, too, was dissected and viewed in terms of the passing flux of thoughts, impulses, perceptions, and sensations of which it is constituted. No essence was held up as inherently nobler, purer, or more real than this bag of decaying flesh. The monk's goal in reflecting on the body was to become more mindful of it, not to withdraw from it. The ascetic flavor of early Buddhist texts should not mislead us. Never is matter presented as inherently dangerous or as less real than consciousness. Pleasures of the flesh that stimulate our craving are to be shunned, but so are rigid views and judgments.

Indeed, the body is more innocent than our mental attachments. Of the four kinds of craving described in the Mahanidana Sutra—"grasping at sense objects . . . speculative opinions . . . rule and ritual . . . theories of the soul"—only one is physical. Only one involves sense desire or bodily appetite.

The Buddha himself was derided by his early ascetic companions for indulging, rather than punishing the flesh in his pursuit of enlightenment. Like them, he had mortified the body in grueling austerities. The hunger, filth, and exhaustion he inflicted on himself has been vividly portrayed in Buddhist art. Then, before he sat down under the bodhi tree, a woman saw his emaciated state and offered him a meal of rice and milk. To the scorn of his former associates, he accepted it.

Later he described how his acceptance of that meal caused the yogis to "turn on me in disgust, saying the recluse Gautama has reverted to a life of abundance." When he went to preach to them after his enlightenment, they initially refused to salute him. But the teachings they received transformed their understanding of reality and thus launched the Buddhist movement.

Sujata, the woman who brought food to Gautama, is honored in carvings throughout the Buddhist world. Kneeling with her bowl beneath the lotus throne, she serves as a reminder that the body is not to be despised as less real or less worthy than mind.

Larger Body, Larger Mind

If consciousness co-arises with form, can we limit it to the human realm? Is it the unique possession of our species? Does it set us apart from the rest of the phenomenal world?

The Dharma says no. Consciousness pervades all forms of existence. Its teachings can begin to free us from the anthropocentrism we have inherited from the Abrahamic religions.

The English-born monk and scholar Sangharakshita notes that in Buddhism the human is but "one manifestation of a current of psychophysical energy, manifesting now as god, now as animal, etc." He points out that this belief in psychic continuity underlies the compassion for all beings, the "boundless heart" that the Buddha exemplified.

Consciousness is throughout, but it is not unitary. It is not some universal essence or glue—the eternal oneness we find in Hinduism. There the omnipresence of Brahman, or the pervasiveness of Vishnu, remains changeless and enduring behind the screen of illusion. There, to gain awareness of this supernal consciousness, we must strip away the material particularities of life forms.

But in the Buddhadharma, where consciousness co-arises with form, it is, in every instance, particular. It is characterized not by sameness, but by its own unique presence, its "thatness" or "suchness," called *tathata* in Sanskrit.

All worlds and planes of existence teem with consciousness. Our minds can perceive connection with all life forms and learn from them, as the Buddha did with elephant, rabbit, serpent, and many others, referring to them in terms of earlier incarnations. Not only seers and shamans, but scientists also, have revealed the capacity of the human spirit to know and be informed by its connectedness with other life forms. The will to do this is a gift and saving grace. For human mentality presents a distinctive feature: the capacity for choice. To be human, to win a human birth, brings the option of changing one's karma. That is why, in Buddhist teachings, a human life is considered so rare and priceless a privilege. And that is why Buddhist practice, in venerable traditions, begins with meditation on the precious opportunity that a human existence provides: the opportunity to wake up for the sake of all beings.

The Dharma vision of a co-arising world, alive with consciousness, is a powerful inspiration for the healing of the Earth. It helps us see three important things. First, it shows us how profoundly we're entangled in the web of life, thus relieving us of our human arrogance and loneliness. Second, it frees us from having to have it all figured out ahead of time, for the solutions arise as we walk the path and meet each other on the road. And, lastly, it reveals our distinctiveness as humans: our capacity to choose.

SELF AND SOCIETY   3

Our own pulse beats in every stranger's throat.
—BARBARA DEMING

FTER SUPPER at a rural community center, half a dozen visitors stood and talked by the fire. We had enjoyed a delicious meal of fresh, home-grown produce. Conversation turned to our lives in the city and the lack of easy access to food that is not irradiated, adulterated with additives, or contaminated with pesticides. In many low-income neighborhoods there is little to no access to healthy food at all. We shared our discouragement.

A woman who had quietly joined our group and listened to our tales, spoke up. "The best thing to do," she said, "is take control of your own life. Leave the polluted air of the city. Drink pure spring water. Eat organic produce that you have grown yourself or know firsthand is safe." And I imagined there was an embarrassed defiance in her voice when she said, firmly, "That's all we can do now, take care of ourselves."

I listened to her attentively, hearing the logic of her statement. The urban activists among us had adopted it to some extent, installing water purifying systems in our kitchens, shopping at farmers' markets, and subscribing to community supported agriculture boxes that deliver fresh-from-the-farm fruits and vegetables to your door. But her logic made curious our efforts to change the status quo and challenge its institutions. She seemed to believe that she could separate herself from society and declare independence from the world at large.

I groped in vain for a simple comment that could convey what I had glimpsed in the Buddha's teaching of dependent co-arising. It has to do with our relationship to the institutions and the destitute of our society, an inter-existence so real that we cannot escape it by going to live in the country and growing our own food.

The institutions of our society co-arise with us. They are not independent structures separate from our inner lives, like some backdrop to our personal dramas. Nor are they merely projections of our own minds. As collective forms of our ignorance, fears, and greed, they acquire their own momentum, enlist our massive obedience, and depend on our collective consent.

Pouring over early Buddhist scriptures, I appreciated the novelty of these teachings, and their daring. The prevailing view of things in the Buddha's time was very different. The Brahmanic worldview, which dominated most discourse, saw social systems as preordained, divinely created at the beginning of our world. The institution of caste, for example, embodies the cosmic act by which the godhead in the form of the *Mahapurusha,* or Primordial Person, created the world out of his vast body. From his head, trunk, and limbs issued the major caste divisions. Hence the divine right of kings, the innate role of priests, and the fixed, subordinate functions of the lower castes.

In radical contrast to this view, the Buddha saw all social structures as impermanent, contingent products of human interaction, and as revealing the law of dependent co-arising. He illustrated this in the Aggañña Sutta, a discourse so popular that it resurfaces again and again in canonical and post-canonical writings and even in the preamble to the first Burmese constitution. It is the Buddha's fanciful genesis story, his tongue-in-cheek recounting of the beginnings of things and origins of institutions. Remember, as you read this summary of the sutra, that in pretending to know the ultimate source of all things, the Buddha was also poking fun at such metaphysical conjectures.

The Buddha's Creation Story

In the beginning of a world cycle, neither beings nor their world had solid form or distinctive features. Weightless, luminous, and identical, the beings wafted about over a dark and watery expanse. When a frothy substance appeared on the waters, they tasted it. It was delicious, and for its sweet, honey flavor a craving arose.

As the beings consumed more and more, both they and their world changed, both becoming more distinct. The beings began to lose their identical luminosity, and as they did, sun, moon, and stars appeared, bringing with them the alternation of day and night. The beings began to solidify and vary in appearance.

Pride and vanity arose as they compared their beauty, and the savory froth vanished. The beings bewailed its loss: "Ah, the savor of it!" In its place, on an earth that was now firmer, mushroom-like growths appeared of similar tastiness—only to disappear as the creatures fattened on them and changed. The mushrooms were replaced by vines; and these, in turn, by rice.

With every new growth the beings craved and ate, and they became more substantial and diverse. At each stage their use of the natural world modified it, engendered more solidity and new forms of vegetation, and with such usage they themselves altered, developing more and more distinctive features. In this interaction both creatures and world progressively differentiated, each gaining in solidity and variety.

When rice first grew, it was without husk, and after being harvested, would grow again in a day. A lazy person, to save effort, decided to harvest two meals at once. Soon all beings were harvesting for two days at a time, then four days, then eight. With this new practice of hoarding, the rice changed: a husk appeared around the grain and the cut stem did not grow again. It stood only as dry stubble. So the people divided and fenced the land, setting boundaries to ensure their private source of food.

Soon a greedy one took rice from a neighboring plot. Admonished by the others, he promised to refrain, but he took again, repeatedly. Since admonishment was of no avail, he was beaten. In such fashion, with the institution of private property, arose theft and lying and abuse and violence.

Soon such acts were so rampant, the scene so chaotic, that the people decided to select one of their own to act on their behalf—"to be wrathful when indignation is right and to censure what rightly should be censured"—and to receive in return for this service a portion of rice. So arose the *Mahasammata,* the great elected one, and with his rule order prevailed.

Such is the origin of kingship and the warrior class; and so also evolved, by the assumption and differentiation of roles, the other major divisions of society: the Brahmins, Vaisyas, and Sudras. Class and caste were not established by divine fiat; they developed from the interactions of beings like ourselves. They were circumstantial in origin.

This fanciful creation story is humanity's first known expression of a theory of social contract. Government begins with the people, a result of their banding together by choice. The Mahasammata was not divinely appointed and anointed, but was chosen by his peers to act in their stead and serve their purposes.

The kind of causality at play here shows how different the Buddhist concept is from the Western notion of social contract associated with Locke and Rousseau. In the Western concept, individuals who band together to create institutions remain basically unaltered by their association. In dependent co-arising, however, self, society, and world are *all* changed by their interaction. We form relationships and are in turn affected by them.

Social Inclusiveness

The causal dynamics conveyed in the Aggañña Sutta underlie the Buddha's social, economic, and political teachings. They are basic to his rejection of caste discrimination and the egalitarian composition of the Sangha; his distrust of private property and the establishment of voluntary poverty, sharing, and alms-begging in the Sangha; his advocacy of government by assembly and consensus; and the Sangha's rules for debate and the settlement of differences.

The Buddha acknowledged that discrimination and oppression shaped the scope and character of people's lives, but he never conceded that such conditions foreclosed their capacity to live nobly and achieve enlightenment. He delivered this teaching whenever he was questioned about the obvious diversity his Sangha displayed. Many well-born contemporaries were puzzled and even shocked that the Buddha welcomed into his order followers from all strata of society, including merchants, runaway soldiers, and slaves. Brahmin priests heaped "copious and characteristic abuse" on their peers who joined the Sangha, and reviled the Sangha itself for opening its doors to "the vulgar rich, the swarthy skinned and the menials." As Jesus did, the Buddha saw pride in social rank as a spiritual obstacle. As quoted in the Ambattha Sutta, he said "Whoever is in bondage to the notions of birth or lineage, or to pride in social position or connection by marriage, is far from wisdom and righteousness."

Political Participation

In contrast to the Brahmanical notion of a divinely predetermined and eternally valid system of government, the Buddha presented political institutions as human-made and transient, subject to the law of dependent co-arising. It is not surprising that unlike other wandering religious teachers of his period, he often taught in the precincts of cities and the peripheries of political power.

Gautama had grown up in a tribal republic to the north of the two monarchies in which he taught. Such republics had been self-governed by a council or assembly, called a Sangha. When, years later, he established his own monastic order, he called it by the same name (Sangha). From the outset, it was more of an alternative community than a retreat from the world.

The order arose, of course, as a vehicle for the transmission of teachings and a locus for the restructuring of consciousness through meditation. But it represented as well an embodiment of his social ideals. It served as a model for social equality, democratic process, and economic sharing. Inspired by the ancient tribal councils, decisions in the new monastic order were made by consensus, "in concord." Scriptural passages such as the following represent the first references in Indian history to rule by assembly.

> So long, O Bhikkhus, as the brethren foregather often, and frequent the formal meetings of their Order—so long as they meet together in concord, and rise in concord, and carry out in concord the duties of the Order . . . so long may the brethren be expected not to decline, but to prosper.

Repression of beliefs was not to be tolerated, so a rule of schism or *Sanghabheda* was instituted, in which members who disagreed with a Sangha's emphasis or interpretation of the teachings could simply form a new settlement within the larger order. Within each settlement, select groups or committees, each having its own jurisdiction and procedural rules, were established to deal with matters administrative and doctrinal. The expression of varying opinions in the *Sanghakammas*, or assemblies for decision-making, was facilitated by the taking of ballots (*salaka*), again the first recorded use of such procedure in the political history of India.

Since respect for alternative views was more important than ideological solidarity and centralized authority, the Sangha split into many schools. This proliferation of forms testifies to their strength and resilience. Given the endurance of the Buddhadharma over two and a half millennia, it would appear that it hardly required the centralized authority so often deemed necessary for the preservation of religion. Without a Rome or Jerusalem, Buddhism flowered in its diversity of forms, while repeatedly renewing, through study and action, its roots in the teachings of the Buddha.

Economic Sharing

In the Buddha's Dharma and Sangha, we see the kinds of economic concepts and practices that emerge when self and society are seen as interdependent. We see at work the values of non-attachment, generosity, and right livelihood.

The Buddha's teaching that suffering stems from craving (the second Noble Truth) places a high value on self-restraint and low consumption. The traditional mendicant way of the monastic, modeled after the Buddha, embodies the conviction that freedom does not derive from wealth or the satisfaction of appetite. Liberation can be won from the insatiable greed to possess and consume, and from the objects, thoughts, and habits that stimulate that wanting. Possessions, furthermore, are dangerous to the extent that they foster the notion of "mineness" (*mamatta*), and thus encourage belief in a permanent, separate self who possesses. In the Aggañña Sutta, as we saw, the institution of private property is presented as the occasion for the arising of theft, lying, and violence. From this perspective, the goal of modern advertising, to induce the sensation of need and the desire to acquire, is immoral. For that matter, so is an economic system dependent on ever-widening public consumption of nonessential commodities and artifacts.

As an antidote to attachment and the delusion it engenders, the Buddha preached generosity (*dana*) and organized a community in which private property was renounced; all goods were shared in common. The Sangha comprised as its members *bhikkhus* and *bhikkhunis*, terms which literally mean not monk and nun, but "sharesman" and "shareswoman," one who receives a share of something. Their alms-begging was not just a handy means of subsistence. It was sacramental in nature, betokening relinquishment of personal wealth and trustful reliance on social relations.

The bhikkhus' relation to lay society was symbiotic. In return for material support, the monks and nuns provided counsel, delivered teachings, and exemplified the ideals they taught. They offered laypeople the opportunity to experience their own generosity through the giving of alms. In later centuries, the Sangha's reciprocity included hospitals and orphanages maintained by the bhikkhus, as well as the erection of monuments, libraries, and universities. From the gifts it received, the Sangha created a rich heritage of art and learning.

In the Buddha's teachings, economic sharing is held out as an ideal for relations between laypersons as well as bhikkhus, and a prerequisite of a healthy society. While restraint in consumption is seen as salutary, the condition of poverty is not. The Buddha rejected mortification of the flesh, and affirmed the rightful claims of this body "born of the great elements." Poverty tends to foment desire and attachment. As the Buddha said: A person cannot listen to the Dharma on an empty stomach.

In early Buddhism, there is no vicarious salvation. We are enjoined to be lamps unto ourselves. The responsibility of the individual to work out his or her own liberation requires an economics of sufficiency. An ideal social order, therefore, ensures that everyone has the necessary economic base for his or her spiritual development. An array of sutras and Jataka tales portray the wise ruler as engaging in broad public works and providing jobs, food, and shelter to the needy.

These scriptures express the economic interdependence between the state and its citizenry, and the extent to which its health and security is a function of the well-being of all its people. When the king, in the Kutadanta Sutta, desires to offer a great ritual sacrifice to ensure his future welfare, he is reminded of lawless elements that trouble his realm, pillaging towns and making roads unsafe. His chaplain, who is identified as the Buddha himself in a former life, argues that neither fresh taxation nor punishment of the miscreants will end the disorder. The most effective solution is to create productive employment opportunities: to give food and seed-corn to the farmers, capital to those who would engage in trade, and food and wages to those who would enter government service. Then "those men, following each his own business, will no longer harass the realm." And, according to the story, not only did that happen, but with the advent of peace and security, the state's revenues increased.

In the Mahasudassana Sutta, the king "of greatest glory" is described and his magnificence is reflected in the facilities he creates for the comfort of his people. Many a Jataka tale presents the wise ruler as ministering to his realm in a similar fashion, offering resources that serve not only humans, but beasts and birds as well. For all hangs together, and when the king is unrighteous that seeps through society, infecting ministers and townspeople alike. Even the sun, moon, and stars go wrong in their course.

This concern for the commons was most notably demonstrated in the reign of the Buddhist king Ashoka. As his pillar and rock edicts attest, numerous public works were instituted: roads, wells, hostels, hospitals. These are the first social services on historical record.

> Moreover I have had banyan trees planted on the roads to give shade to man and beast; I have planted mango groves, and I have had ponds dug and shelters erected along the roads at every eight kos. Everywhere I have had wells dug for the benefit of man and beast. . . . What I have done has been done that man may conform to the Dhamma.

The inherent right to worthwhile work is reflected in the concept of "right livelihood," an ingredient of the Buddha's Eightfold Path. According to the teaching of dependent co-arising, the work a person performs not only expresses his character, but modifies it in turn. High value, therefore, must be placed on the nature of this work. Instead of being considered as a necessary evil to which one is condemned, or "disutility" as in classical economics, work is a vehicle for the creation and expression of our deepest values.

Meaningful employment is more important than the goods it produces. By linking the person to her fellow beings in reciprocal relationship, and enhancing her self-respect, the value of her work is beyond monetary measure. Labor policies and production plans that view work solely in terms of pay or profit, degrade it and rob it of meaning. High wages, high dividends, increased production or unemployment payments cannot compensate for the human loss that occurs when assembly-line techniques or joblessness deprive a worker of developing and enjoying her skills.

Ends and Means

As has been repeatedly affirmed throughout human history, moral considerations pertain not only to the goals we try to achieve, but also to the manner in which we go about trying to achieve them. Frequently these appear at odds with each other, like the "war to end all wars." We all are familiar with the moral anguish that arises when worthy objectives seem only attainable by acts which appear, by their nature, to compromise them.

The conflict between ends and means arises from a dichotomized way of thinking, which leads us to imagine that the goal "out there" has an existence independent of ourselves or the methods we employ. Aristotle assumed this to be the case, when he explained his concept of final cause (*telos*). It is that for the sake of which one acts. In his Nichomachean Ethics, he said: "Wherever there are certain ends over and above the actions themselves, it is [their] nature . . . to be better than the activities." The goal, then, appears as more real and more valuable than the activities leading to it; and these activities appear as merely instrumental to an end whose nature is more final and complete.

Such presuppositions lead to instrumentalist ways of thinking, where concern for ends overrides considerations of the ethical appropriateness of the means. Such considerations come to appear as moral niceties, welcome where they can be accommodated, but in the last analysis, "when push comes to shove," the means are irrelevant to the goal in view. So we found ourselves attempting to bomb the world into peace.

The Dharma of dependent co-arising turns this kind of thinking inside out. It asserts, as have many saints and teachers over the ages, that the goal is not something "out there," aloof from our machinations, but rather a function of the way itself, interdependent with our acts. As doer and deed are interconnected. As his own thoughts and actions are modified, so are his objectives. For however he articulates these objectives, they reflect his present perceptions and interpretations of reality, which are altered, however slightly, by every cognitive event. Means are not subordinate to ends so much as creative of them—they are ends-in-the-making. As Audre Lorde said, "The master's tools will never dismantle the master's house." They can only perpetuate it.

The Buddha offered the Dharma, not as a goal to be reached so much as a Way (*magga*). Each step on this way is of intrinsic value, the Dharma being "glorious in the beginning, glorious in the middle, glorious at the end." Value is intrinsic to each act because action, karma, is what we are and what we become. Although we are summoned to strive to transform our lives and our consciousness, we do so with the paradoxical knowledge that, though we may feel very far from where we want to be, there is no place to get to; for we are already there. This religious paradox, manifest in many faiths, overturns the problem of ends and means. It shows that the goals we pursue are not distant from us in time or space, but present realities, unfolding out of the core of our existence and capable of transforming in the moment.

We can never avoid what we seek to escape, least of all the political and economic institutions into which we are born. But by virtue of their dependence on our participation, by vote or speak-out, lobby or boycott, they can change. They mirror our truest intentions. This is what I would have liked to say to the woman who joined us by the fire that night in the country, because it is what I hear the Buddha's teaching saying to me.

Karma: The Co-arising of Doer and Deed

4

We build the road and the road builds us.

—SARVODAYA MOVEMENT IN SRI LANKA

THE BUDDHA'S TEACHING OF *anatta,* that there is no separate and permanent self, is a keystone of the Dharma. When I began to register the meaning of this teaching, I felt a tremendous release. I sensed how it could liberate me from habits of self-concern. It promised freedom to act—freedom to do what is to be done, without endlessly taking my own spiritual and psychological pulse before getting on with it.

I received early lessons in anatta from my first meditation teacher, Sister Karma Khechog Palmo, an English-born, Tibetan Buddhist nun in India. When I made statements like "I cannot sit still" or "I am lazy (or angry or stupid)," she would immediately cut me short. "Stop!" she'd say, "Stop saying 'I' in that way, when talking about your experience." Such "I" statements work like cement, lending a kind of permanence to passing feelings. Sister Palmo pointed out that it is more accurate and helpful to say, "Anger is happening," or "Fears are arising."

Her admonishments helped me recognize the burden of a solidified self—and the burden began to lift. The "Joanna" who kept looking in the mirror to check her rightness or worthiness or guilt, seemed to dissolve a little. But the teaching of anatta can seem, at first approach, to free us from conventional morality as well.

Nance, a young woman I knew, had been recently exposed to Buddhist ideas. She was leaving a hotel after a conference, when her suitcase fell open. Along with her clothes and cosmetics, a set of the hotel's towels spilled out on the lobby floor. With an embarrassed shrug, she handed the towels to the bellboy and proceeded out the door. Her horrified roommate asked her if she wasn't ashamed of herself. "What self?" said Nance. "You only get uptight about this if you believe in the self. At least I am free of *that* illusion."

Her comment may sound blithe, or silly, but it highlights an issue in Buddhist thought that has been problematic for many. What is there to get uptight about, if we are but a passing flow of psychophysical events? Does it matter what we do? Are we accountable for our acts? These questions have puzzled some Buddhist scholars too, especially in the West. Pointing out apparent contradictions between the doctrine of anatta and the ethical exhortations of the Buddha, a number have concluded that it weakens any notion of personal accountability.

The basic issue here is the connection between what we do and what we are. Or, if we understand our existence in terms of our conscious participation in reality, the question is whether our acts affect that participation—that is, our capacity to know, choose, and enjoy. If not, then notions of responsibility are tangential to one's life, noble but inconsequential. If they do, then distinctions between the pragmatic and the moral dissolve. In the Buddhist perspective of dependent co-arising, this is the case. What we do not only matters, it molds us.

The Teaching of Karma

The concept of karma is often associated with belief in rebirth or reincarnation, a belief that was almost universally accepted in the culture of the Buddha's time. Many questions addressed to the Buddha concerning the course of the spiritual life, and particularly the moral effect of deeds, were posed within the context of this widely held belief. The teaching of no-self raised problems: If the self is transient, how can it survive from one life to the next? And how can it be affected by previous lives?

Actually, the Buddha did not consider it useful to reflect on the possibility and character of other lifetimes. To seek one's past identities can obscure the understanding of dependent co-arising. He said that if you really understand this causal law, you won't run back to the past thinking:

> Did I live in times gone by? Or did I not? What was I in times gone by? How was I then? Or free from being what? . . . Or [running to the future] think, Shall I be reborn in a future time, or shall I not? What shall I become in the future? . . . These questions never arise, brethren, if by right insight, [you] have seen things as they really are in this causal happening, this paticca samuppada.

Yet, even focusing on this present life, disciples often queried the Buddha as to who is responsible for the habits, sufferings, and pleasures we experience. In reply, he refused to say that they are caused by a past actor with whom we have no more connection. One cannot categorically separate the "I" who experiences the result from the "I" who set it in motion; for they are not discontinuous. Yet neither are they the same. One cannot say that "one and the same person both acts and experiences the result," for the person is different, altered. There *is* a continuity, but it is not the continuity of an agent as a distinct and enduring being. The continuity resides in the acts themselves that condition consciousness and feelings in dependent co-arising. It inheres in the reflexive dynamics of action, shaping that which brought it forth.

For action, the term karma is used. Early on, in pre-Buddhist literature, the word denoted ritual acts; then by extension it meant religiously ordained social duties. In the Buddhist texts, it is broadened to include all volitional behavior—bodily, verbal, and mental. This is what we are. As Pali scholar T. W. Rhys Davids pointed out, "Where others said 'soul,' Gautama said 'action.'"

Our present psychophysical structure is not that of a continuing self-identical entity, nor is it discontinuous from our past selves. Using the term *kaya,* which often included speech and thought along with body, the Buddha said: This kaya, brethren, is not your own, neither is it that of any others. It should be regarded as brought about by actions of the past, by plans, by volitions, by feelings."

The effect of our behavior is inescapable, not because God watches and tallies, or an angel marks our acts in a ledger, but because our acts co-determine what we become.

They do so by means of the volitional formations. These habits and inclinations condition the ways in which we interpret and react to things. The term *sankhara* means "put together," "compounded," "organized." Sankharas accrue from previous volitional acts and represent the reflexive or recoil effects of those actions—the tendencies they create, the habits they perpetuate.

Because the character of a person's experience is affected by these formations, his identity is inseparable from what he does and thinks, has done and thought. He is neither aloof from these acts, nor their victim. They are his identity, continuity, and resource, as the *Anguttara Nikaya* declares:

> My action is my possession,
> my action is my inheritance,
> my action is the womb which bears me,
> my action is my refuge.

Liberation of the Will

Highly deterministic notions of karma were current in the Buddha's time. The Jains, for example, taught that every single act, regardless of circumstance, inexorably bears its fruit. No spiritual progress can be made without personally undergoing all the consequences. Set in motion by the physical effects of deeds, karma represents a kind of substance or film, an obscuring accumulation that can only be worn away through expiation. This process of wearing away can be hastened by mortification of the flesh. The Ajivika view, also taught in the

Buddha's time, is even more deterministic. Considering *every* aspect of present experience, mental and physical, as the result of past action, it sees any human effort whatever as fruitless.

Lama Govinda vividly evokes the grim fatalism of these notions of karma, where the past rules the present with a heavy hand:

> The idea that the consequence of all deeds, whether of a mental or corporeal kind, must be tasted to the very last morsel, and that through every most trivial action, through the slightest motion of the heart, one is further involved in the inextricable net of fate, is assuredly the most frightful specter that the human heart, or more correctly the human intellect, has ever conjured up.

In contrast, he points out, the doctrine of paticca samuppada frees us from fatalism "at every moment." The effects of the past are not cast in concrete, because the sankharas themselves can be altered by present intentions and actions.

If karma cannot be changed, the Buddha said, "all effort is fruitless." This he would not allow. He rejected determinist views of karma because of their crippling effect on human will. They provide, he said, "neither the desire to do, nor the effort to do, nor the necessity to do this deed or abstain from that deed. So then, the necessity for action or inaction [is] not found to exist in truth or verity."

The "desire to do, and effort to do,"—in other words our volition—modifies the effects of our past, and broadens the scope for present endeavor. This emphasis on will is the most distinctive feature of the Buddhist concept of karma. The Buddha said, "Where there have been deeds, Ananda, personal weal and woe are in consequence of the will there was in the deeds."

That is why the sankharas, which condition our perceptions and cognitions, are understood as "volitional formations." Shaped by our desires, they carry forward the energy of the will. The power inherent in past acts resides in the choices that produced them. A human existence is considered to be incomparably precious because intention is so important and choice so consequential. Beings in other realms of the wheel of life, such as animals, ghosts, and gods, experience pain and pleasure, but only the human can alter experience through decision. Given the astronomical number of other forms of life, this human opportunity is extraordinarily rare and valuable.

Since will determines the effect of actions, for good or for grief, it must be mobilized. Exertion is required. The early scriptures abound in exhortations to vigorous effort. Buddhist practitioners are summoned repeatedly by the scriptures to be "intent on vigilance" and "of stirred up energy, self-resolute, with mindfulness aroused." One of the cardinal failings, is *thinamiddham,* sloth or lethargy. By the same token, *viriya,* (to be understood as energy, resolution, vigor) is seen as essential to enlightenment and a cardinal virtue in its own right. This energy is a vivid contrast to the passivity and fatalism popularly associated with the notion of karma. Here will is primary, and it can be trained.

> Wherefore, brethren, thus must ye train yourselves: liberation of the will through love we will develop, we will often practice it, we will make it a vehicle and a base, take our stand upon it, store it up, thoroughly set it going.

In the early Buddhist view, then, a person's identity resides not in an enduring self but in her actions—that is, in the choices that shape these actions. Because the dispositions formed by previous choices can be modified in turn by present behavior, one's identity as choice-maker is fluid, one's experience alterable. Affected by the past, one's identity can also break free of the past.

The Systems View of Karma

Systems theory has helped me understand this. From that perspective as well, what we do shapes what we are. Because the open system is self-organizing, its behavior cannot be dictated from without. External pressures can do no more than interact with the system's internal organization. Since a person's actions derive from her unique observations and reflections, she can always choose. Though her reactions are conditioned by previous experience, present circumstances bring ever-new perceptions and opportunities. As systems-oriented political scientist Karl Deutsch says, "The cognitive system is changing and remaking with each decision in the present."

> Thanks to what it has learned in the past, it is not wholly subject to the present. Thanks to what it still can learn, it is not wholly subject to the past. Its internal rearrangements in response to each new challenge are made by the interplay between its present and its past.

Meta-level reflections arise, bringing awareness of other choices that could be made; and because they do, the individual could always have acted otherwise. Deutsch goes on to say:

> Each of us is responsible for what he is now, for the personality he himself has acquired by his past actions. Nor are we wholly prisoners of any one decision or any one experience. Ordinarily, it takes many repetitions so to stalk a mind with memories and habits that at long last lead to the same city, whether it be taken, in religious language, as the City of Destruction, or the City of Salvation.

One is struck by the parallels to the Buddhist idea of karma and especially the sankharas, the memories and habits that "stock the mind" and incline us to repeat them. The systems view, like the Buddhist, does not see us as victims of our past, hapless pawns of forces and times beyond our reach. Rather, as Deutsch continues:

> It sees in the actual moment of decision only a dénouement in which we reveal to ourselves and to others what we have

already become thus far. Each step on the road to "heaven" or to "hell," to harmonious autonomy or to disintegration, was marked by a free decision. . . . The determinate part of our behavior is the stored result of our past free decisions.

Choice is so important because it actually constitutes what it means to be a person. To systems-psychologist O. H. Mowrer, choice defines consciousness itself.

The eternal question is, "What to do? How to act?" And consciousness, as I conceive it, is the operation whereby information is continuously received, evaluated, and summarized in the form of "decisions," "choices," and "intentions."

Through the operation of feedback, the behaviors we adopt and the goals we pursue take root in the psyche. They affect the ways we interpret experience—and these ways constitute who we are. Doer and deed co-arise. Hence our continuity of character, bearing the stamp of repeated choice and habit. Hence also our freedom, for new options arise with each present act of will.

Here then is the answer to our question, "Does it matter what we do?" It matters to the extent that *we* matter. Indeed, our acts matter—incarnate—in us, for they make us what we are. Though we fall into feelings of overwhelm or hopelessness, we can still choose to see what is possible.

This spells both grief and promise for the self we tend to posit and on whose behalf we tend to act. Because it is altered by each act, wise or foolish, fearful or brave, the self, even as decision-maker, is doomed as an enduring entity. Constantly changing, it arises and passes. Yet in that very evanescence lies promise. For in the flow of perception and response, choices can be made that open broader vistas to discern and know, wider opportunities to love and to act.

MOTHER OF ALL BUDDHAS   5

Whenever I hear
the edgeless sound
in the deep night
O Mother!
I find you again.
—KYOZAN JOSHU

ABOUT FIVE CENTURIES AFTER the Buddha, the Wheel of the Dharma, they say, turned again. The Buddha's central teaching of dependent co-arising was reaffirmed and clothed in fresh language and imagery. This turning is represented by scriptures called Perfection of Wisdom, or Prajñaparamita, which herald the advent of Mahayana Buddhism.

Here the hero figure of the bodhisattva appears, no longer solely identified with former lives of the Buddha, but with all beings who perceive the interdependent nature of reality. And here that marvelous insight itself is personified. Emerging in the same era as did her Mediterranean counterpart Sophia, this embodiment of wisdom is female. She is the Perfection of Wisdom, the Mother of All Buddhas.

She presents an archetypal structure very different from the feminine attributes we have inherited from patriarchal thought. Freed from the dichotomies that oppose earth to sky, flesh to spirit, the feminine appears clothed in light and space. She is that pregnant zero point where the illusion of ego is lost and the world, no longer feared, is re-entered with compassion.

To get acquainted with her and learn more about the wisdom of interbeing, let us look at one of the richest of the scriptures that honor her, the Perfection of Wisdom in 8000 Lines, written down some two thousand years ago.

A Different Kind of Wisdom

> As Buddhas, world teachers
> Compassionate, are your sons,
> So you, O blessed one, are
> Grandmother of all beings.
> . . . He who sees you is liberated,
> And he who does not see you is liberated, too.

The texts that bear her name are central to all major developments in later Buddhism, from Madhyamika philosophy to Vajrayana and Zen. These sutras reiterate her categorical difference from earlier and more conventional notions of wisdom.

In the scriptures of the Pali Canon, wisdom was featured, along with moral conduct and meditation, as one of the three essential aspects of the Path, and seen as the knowledge of dependent co-arising. This doctrine had been primarily understood in terms of the non-substantiality of the self. The self was perceived as a congruence of aggregates, and these in turn as a series of events, or units of experience, known as *dharma*s. As scholastic Buddhism developed, the nature of these dharmas became a primary focus of attention. To understand the flux of dharmas, from which the illusion of self arose, became a matter of importance and some fascination. Dharmas were conceptualized, listed, typed, and classified. Differing views on their nature and interaction engendered different schools of thought. Wisdom became, in short, a rational and analytic exercise, comprising enumeration, categorization, and speculative theory. The debates threatened to go on endlessly when from the wings a new wisdom moved onto the scene.

Because she pointed to a reality which eludes classifications, this wisdom, *prajña,* was called *paramita,* which means "gone beyond" or to the "other side," as well as "perfection." To those who were dryly and doggedly analyzing the dharmas, she offered not theories, but paradoxes. "Countless beings do I lead to Nirvana and yet there are none who are led to Nirvana." "The bodhisattva will go forth—but he will not go forth to anywhere." "In the Buddha's teachings he trains, (but) no training is this training and no one is trained." "In his jubilation he transforms all dharmas, but none are transformed, for dharmas are illusory."

No formula captured her insight, but through the paradoxes shone a light offering release from the self-adhesive nature of human logic. The self is non-substantial, and so also are its concepts, the very dharmas into which the self was analyzed. They are as empty as the self, existing only in relation to it. Thus does Perfection of Wisdom return to the Buddha's quintessential doctrine, the radical interdependence of all things.

In the text it is Sariputra, traditionally revered as the Buddha's most learned disciple, who represents the scholastic mentality. Weighted with logic and literalness, he struggles with the apparent contradictions of the new wisdom, and asks questions that are answered by the Buddha and Subhuti, a follower who is now raised up as an example of one who sees into the co-dependently arising nature of things. The paradoxes, as Sariputra learns, leave the observing ego with no safe place to stand. They knock away the concepts that perpetuate it.

This wisdom, then, is not the kind one can think oneself into. It is a way of seeing. Without it, the very practice of virtue and meditation can be an ego prop, to which we cling in pride or desperation. With it, the world itself (*samsara*) is altered—not suppressed or rejected, but transfigured.

Clear Light, Deep Space

> The Buddhas in the world-systems in the ten directions
> bring to mind this perfection of wisdom as their mother.
> The Saviors of the world who were in the past, and also are
>   now in the ten directions,
> have issued from her, and so will the future ones be.
> She is the one who shows this world [for what it is],
> she is the genetrix, the mother of the Buddhas.

The mother, like the wisdom she offers, is elusive. She is barely personalized in the sutra; no stories attach to her, no direct speech is accorded her, no physical descriptions of her are offered. None of the gestures, colors, or adornments that will figure in the images made of her centuries later are presented. The dozen or so epithets for her in our sutra appear mostly in passing, as if self-explanatory—"Prajña-paramita, the mother," "Mother of the Tathagatas," "Mother of the Sugatas," "Mother of the bodhisattvas," "instructress of the Tathagatas in this world," "genetrix and nurse of the six perfections."

As children revere the mother who brought them forth, so

> fond are the Buddhas of the Perfection of Wisdom, so much
> do they cherish and protect it. For she is their mother and
> begetter, she showed them this all-knowledge, she instructed
> them in the ways of the world. . . . All the Tathagatas, past,
> future and present, win full enlightenment, thanks to her.

The feminine character of this wisdom is conveyed in many analogies. In his eagerness to learn and experience enlightenment, the bodhisattva is likened to "a pregnant woman, all astir with pains, whose time has come for her to give birth." He is "like a mother, ministering to her only child," in his devotion to the welfare of other beings. "Just as a cow does not abandon her young calf," so the teacher continues to guide the bodhisattva until the bodhisattva knows this Perfection of

Wisdom by heart. In his constant pondering of this wisdom, he is like a man who had made a date with a handsome, attractive, and good-looking woman. "And if now that woman were held back by someone else and could not leave her house, what do you think, Subhuti," asks the Buddha, "with what would that man's preoccupations be connected?" "With the woman, of course," Subhuti answers, "he thinks about her coming, about the things they will do together, and about the joy, fun, and delight he will have with her." "Just as preoccupied as such a man," says the Lord, "is the bodhisattva with thoughts of the Perfection of Wisdom."

And when the bodhisattva meets her, what qualities does he find in her? He finds light, emptiness, space, and a samsara-confronting gaze that is both clinical and compassionate.

"The Perfection of Wisdom gives light, O Lord. I pay homage to the Perfection of Wisdom!" cries Sariputra, after listening to Subhuti and the Buddha. "She is a source of light, and from everyone in the triple world she removes darkness. . . . She brings light to the blind, she brings light so that all fear and distress may be forsaken. She has gained the five eyes, and she shows the path to all beings. She herself is an organ of vision."

As light and insight, she reveals that all dharmas are void, signless, and wishless, not-produced, not-stopped, and nonexistent. By the same token, Perfect Wisdom herself is empty (*sunya*). She is "not a real thing." Like dharmas, Buddhas, and bodhisattvas, she offers "no basis for apprehension." The sutra acknowledges that this is fearful to contemplate, and that this teaching is "alarming" and "terrifying." Those who are "not frightened on hearing the Mother's deep tenets," "not cowed, paralyzed, or stupefied," those "who do not despair, turn away, or become dejected," reveal their potential for full Buddhahood.

While Perfection of Wisdom reveals *sunyata,* the void, in all its awesomeness, she seems to recognize the terror it can initially induce, for she also offers comfort. "In her we find defense and protection." "She offers the safety of the wings of enlightenment." "She helps with the four grounds of self-confidence." The reassurance she gives is symbolized in the *abhaya mudra* of her raised right hand, the fear-not gesture that we encounter in some later Tantric images of her.

Her compassion is not seen as a cradling, cuddling, or clasping to the bosom. Rather it inheres in her very seeing and is implicit in her clear-eyed vision of the world's suffering. The many eyes, to which Sariputra referred in connection with her illuminating insight, become symbolic of this compassion. When she assumes the form of Tara, these eyes, set in her forehead, hands, and feet, express her caring. It is not surprising that metaphors of sheltering and enclosing are relatively rare for the Perfection of Wisdom. Since, as the bodhisattva is repeatedly reminded, there is no ground to stand on, the predominant movement is to imagine her in space, in boundless immensity.

In *akasa,* the infinite expanse of space, the notions of light and void conjoin. In this sutra lies the metaphor par excellence for the Perfection of Wisdom. Like space, she is endless (*ananta*). Like space, she is immeasurable, incalculable, and insubstantial; like space, she cannot be increased, decreased, or confined in categories. Like sheer space, she can terrify, but the bodhisattva must plunge right into it, unafraid and ready to delight. If he can trust her, he becomes "like a bird that on its wings courses in the air. It neither falls to the ground, nor does it stand anywhere on any support. It dwells in space, just as in the air, without being either supported or settled therein."

This space, into which the bodhisattva ventures, is not the old realm of the sky gods, traditionally accorded to the male in the mythical dualities of sky father-earth mother. Attributes of the sky father featured the sovereign heights of his heavens, his astronomic regularity and law, the power of his thunderous downpours. No such references are made to the Mother of the Buddhas, no allusions to the majesty, order, or power of heavenly phenomena. The one attribute she shares with him is that of all-seeing. Furthermore, she is not set in opposition to the recumbent earth; on the contrary, she is, on occasion, metaphorically equated with it as ground of being. "As many trees, fruits, flowers as there are have all come out of the earth . . . (so have) the Buddha's offspring and the gods and the dharmas issued from Perfect Wisdom." This wisdom is also linked with earth by the act ascribed to the Buddha during his enlightenment vigil, in which he called her to witness. He reached down and touched her, affirming his right to attain freedom.

The measureless space of the Perfection of Wisdom extends not only outward and up, but also inward and down. It is deep space. "Deep is the Perfection of Wisdom," says Subhuti. And the Lord answers, "Yes, with a depth like that of space."

The Pregnant Zero

A rich and startling dimension is added to the Perfection of Wisdom, when we learn how some of the terms that describe her played a role in the development of mathematics. To be specific, she influenced the emergence of zero. The early numerical system developed by the Babylonians was hampered by having no such concept or symbol. It was Indian mathematicians in the early centuries C.E. who evolved the decimal system and the crucially important notion of zero. All of this, transmitted to the West by Arab traders, became the basis for European numbering and computation.

Culture historian Ananda K. Coomaraswamy has pointed out that in India, previous to numerical notations, verbal symbols were used technically. For the concept of zero, in particular, a variety of terms was employed, and these technical verbal symbols derived from Indian metaphysics. Now, several of these words for zero, such as sunya, akasa, and ananta, turn out to be chief attributes assigned to the Perfection of Wisdom, Mother of all Buddhas.

The apparent opposition between some of the terms used for zero, e.g., *purna* (full) along with sunya (empty), is interpreted by Coomaraswamy to indicate that "to the Indian mind all numbers are virtually or potentially present in that which is without number . . . (or) that zero is to number as possibility is to actuality." He further reflects that the use of ananta (endless) implies an identification of zero with infinity—"the beginning of all series being thus the same as their end." Akasa represents "primarily not a concept of physical space, but of a purely principal space without dimension, though the matrix of dimension."

This zero space becomes the still center of the turning world. *Kha* and *nabha,* two other terms for zero used technically by mathematicians, originally meant the hole in the hub of a wheel through which the axle runs. For the wheel to revolve the center must be empty. Hence, presumably, the sign for zero. It is the circle in which end and beginning merge. It is also a sexual sign for the female, linking the feminine and the void, as does the Perfection of Wisdom. Around the emptiness or sunyata, which she represents, the Wheel of the Dharma turns. That void is, as D. T. Suzuki said, "not an abstraction but an experience, or a deed enacted where there is neither space nor time."

The conjunction of these symbols in the Perfection of Wisdom evokes a similar conjunction in the *Four Quartets* of T. S. Eliot.

> Garlic and sapphires in the mud
> Clot the bedded axle-tree.
>
> At the still point of the turning world
> . . . there the dance is.
>
> We must be still and still moving
> Into a further intensity
>
> For a further union . . .
> In the end is my beginning

Note the Mother's attitude vis-a-vis this world. The liberation offered by the Perfection of Wisdom is not attained by turning away from samsara. "Those who are certain that they have got safely out of this world are unfit for full enlightenment," says her sutra. The light that she bestows does not dazzle, eclipse, or blind one to mundane phenomena and the traffic of beings; but clear and cool, it illumines the world "as it is." The capacity to see reality as it is (*yathabutham*), fully accepting the multiplicities and particularities of things, is repeatedly stressed as a gift of the Mother of All Buddhas. While the world is often presented in the text as dream, illusion, and magic show, one does not shun it—for there is no dharma that is *more* real or in whose pursuit the bodhisattva would lift his gaze from things-as-they-are.

The Mother of the Buddhas, therefore, does not call the bodhisattva beyond this world, to final nirvana. She retains him on this side of reality, for the sake of all beings. "In this dwelling of Perfect Wisdom . . . you shall become a savior of the helpless, a defender of the defenseless . . . a light to the blind, and you shall guide to the path those who have lost it, and you shall become a support to those who are without support." In such passages as these, the bodhisattva path is, for the first time, fully expressed—as a summons to all persons. The skill in means (*upaya*) by which the bodhisattva responds and acts within the realm of contingency and need is seen as essential to his enlightenment. Upaya, the readiness to reach out and improvise, is the other face of wisdom. Together they constitute the ground for ethical action and delight—revalorizing samsara while assigning no fixed reality to its varied manifestations.

Such is the wisdom of the Mother of all Buddhas, empty of preconception, the pregnant point of potential action, beholding the teeming world with a vision that transfigures. When she is later portrayed as Green Tara, her gestures will recall this active, compassionate aspect; for the right arm is outstretched to help, and the right leg, no longer tucked up in the aloof serenity of the lotus posture, extends downward, ready to step into the world.

Neither Temptress nor Trap

To appreciate the distinctiveness of the Perfection of Wisdom, we must see how her symbolization as wisdom, light, and space, runs counter to the feminine archetype prevailing in Hindu culture. There we find a worldview rooted in polarities between earth and sky, nature and consciousness, matter and mind.

The aboriginal pre-Aryan culture centered around worship of a fertility goddess. Like other neolithic societies dependent on agriculture, it worshiped the productivity of nature (seen as female because of its birthing capacity), while recognizing its remorseless vegetative cycle of growth and death. The goddess of the Indus Valley and Dravidian culture was driven underground by the invading Aryans and their chariot-driving warrior sky-gods. Centuries later she resurfaced, clothed in respectability, in the Samkhyan philosophy, which had a profound and formative effect on subsequent Indian thought. Samkhya reestablished her in the form of the eternally evolving and fecund *prakrti* (nature principle). She is dynamic and unconscious, in contrast to *purusa,* the conscious spirit. The individual soul finds himself entrapped in prakrti's turbulent world of change and materiality, and it is only in extricating himself from her that transcendence and release can be won.

The ancient matriarchal element also reasserted itself in the later development of the Devi and her cult. Represented variously as Durga and Kali and other female forms, she is essentially one—Devi, the goddess. Whether adorned with peacock feathers or garlanded with skulls, she is the ceaselessly active one, prakrti, *maya, shakti.* She is the restlessness of primal matter, the fecund and cruel mother. As the creative power of the male gods, from whom she issues, she complements their pure, passive intelligence.

The goddess is both indulgent and terrible. Ambivalent feelings about the mother figure she symbolizes are reflected in the dual status of women in traditional Hindu society. As a sexual partner, the woman often tends to be presented as a dangerous and enfeebling seductress, a semen-stealer; but as a mother—the mother of a son, that is—she is revered and accorded prerogatives denied her as a person. Although birthing a son elevates her status, she is expected to remain ever subservient to him. Consequently, the indulgence that a mother lavishes on her son is not unmixed; as anthropologist Richard Lannoy puts it, "with her feeling of maternal love co-exist feelings of envy and retaliation." Lannoy, studying this phenomenon, links it with the prevalence of "the terrible mother" in Hindu myth, and finds its imagery expressive of both dependence and aggression.

In any event, there are philosophic grounds for this image of the feminine in the Hindu world. Differing apprehensions of reality lie at the root of the contrast between the Devi and the Perfection of Wisdom. A metaphysical dichotomy between consciousness and nature leads to a vision of spirit as struggling to be free from the toils of matter. Matter comes to be seen as polluting and binding, her fertile nature as arbitrary, lavish, cruel.

Jungian psychologist James Hillman shows that a love-hate relationship with matter is endemic in the Great Mother complex and evident today in contemporary values. When the archetypal mother is linked with the earthly in opposition to the psyche, a dual response is elicited from the son or spirit: rebellion and possession. Spirit rebels by subjugating matter, be it by mortification of the flesh or defoliation of the land. It seeks to possess the mother by accumulating and consuming her goods and resources. Either way, matter (*mater*) exerts her power and fascination.

Even when "maya" is understood as derivative of the transcendent One, as in Vedanta, it is perceived as both binding and maternal. As Krishna says in the *Bhagavad Gita* (VII. 14–5): "For all this (nature) is my creative power (maya) . . . hard to transcend. Whoso shall put his trust in me alone shall pass beyond (maya)." Commenting on this passage, scholar R. C. Zaehner says: The spirit "is made flesh in the womb of nature . . . but matter binds; and *like any mother, is unwilling to let her son go free:* hence she does all she can to deceive him; as such she is maya which, at this stage of the language, means both *creative power* and *deceit.*" [Emphasis added.]

The Perfection of Wisdom, Mother of All Buddhas, escapes this role and presents a completely different feminine archetype. The doctrine of dependent co-arising permits no polarization of consciousness and nature. Matter, seen as co-emergent with mind, is neither temptress nor trap. Faith in this wisdom mother is very different, therefore, from devotion accorded to the Devi. The Perfection of Wisdom is not a mother to be placated and cajoled. Faith in her is not a seeking of favors, but a letting go, a falling into emptiness. It is the release of one's clutching onto dharmas and concepts, a venturing outward, a leaning into space. Seeing through the fiction of a separate self, one passes through the zero point. Because such a zero experience is a kind of birth, generative of new worlds, it is fitting that she who leads us through it is seen as "genetrix" and mother.

Centuries later, in profusion of graphic imagery, the Perfection of Wisdom became the prototype of all the female figures featured in Buddhist Tantric interplay. With serene aplomb she copulates with upaya, skill in means. Her "other face," compassionate action, has become her male consort.

Scholars and art lovers have wondered and debated why, in these Buddhist figures, the sexual roles are reversed from the Hindu brand of Tantrism. There in connubial embrace it is Shiva who is the sublimely passive partner, while his consort Shakti represents dynamism. We now understand why the Perfection of Wisdom cannot, without misrepresentation, be equated with Shakti, or even Shiva for that matter. The Buddhist *yab-yum* (mother-father embrace) embodies a different vision altogether.

The fundamental difference is ontological: Perfection of Wisdom is empty, devoid of independent being, whereas Shiva as wisdom is the ultimate essence with which, by aid of Shakti, the adept would merge. In the Hindu pair, maya (material manifestation) is subsumed into *moksha* (spirit and release). In contrast to this, the Tantric symbolism of Buddhism represents not a canceling of one pole, but the continual interplay of both. These poles are not moksha and maya or pure consciousness over or against energy/matter, but rather two kinds of consciousness/energy. In the embrace of prajña and upaya, wisdom and skillful means, life's dialectic modes of vision and action are held in balance, complementary and mutually essential. That numinous copulation reflects the dependent co-arising of all things.

Appearing both as luminous space and compassionate caller of bodhisattvas, Prajñaparamita, the Mother of All Buddhas, conveys a transforming vision of the world. In her and through her the central insight of the Buddha is rediscovered and reaffirmed; and that is why the scriptures that honor her are known as the Second Turning of the Wheel of the Dharma.

PART TWO:

Cultivating the Present

GRATITUDE 6

Just to live is holy,
To be is a blessing.
—RABBI ABRAHAM HESCHEL

WE HAVE RECEIVED an inestimable gift. To be alive in this beautiful, self-organizing universe—to participate in the dance of life with senses to perceive it, lungs that breathe it, organs that draw nourishment from it—is a wonder beyond words. And it is, moreover, an extraordinary privilege to be accorded a human life, with self-reflexive consciousness that brings awareness of our own actions and the ability to make choices. It lets us choose to take part in the healing of our world.

Where We Start

Gratitude for the gift of life is the primary wellspring of all religions, the hallmark of the mystic, the source of all true art. Yet we so easily take this gift for granted. That is why so many spiritual traditions begin with thanksgiving, to remind us that for all our woes and worries, our existence itself is an unearned benefaction, which we could never of ourselves create.

In the Tibetan Buddhist path we are asked to pause before any period of meditative practice and precede it with reflection on the preciousness of a human life. This is not because we as humans are superior to other beings, but because we can "change the karma." In other words, graced with self-reflexive consciousness, we are endowed with the capacity for choice—to take stock of what we are doing and change directions. We may have endured for eons of lifetimes as other life forms, under the heavy hand of fate and the blind play of instinct, but now at last we are granted the ability to consider and judge and make decisions. Weaving our ever more complex neural circuits into the miracle of self-aware-ness, life yearned through us for the ability to know and act and speak on behalf of the larger whole. Now the time has come when by our own choice we can consciously enter the dance.

In Buddhist practice, that first reflection is followed by a second, on the brevity of this precious human life: "Death is certain; the time of death is uncertain." That reflection awakens in us the precious gift of the present moment—to seize this chance to be alive right now on Planet Earth.

Even in the Dark

That our world is in crisis—to the point where survival of conscious life on Earth is in question—in no way diminishes the value of this gift; on the contrary. To us is granted the privilege of being on hand: to take part, if we choose, in the Great Turning to a just and sustain-able society. We can let life work through us, enlisting all our strength, wisdom, and courage, so that life itself can continue.

There is so much to be done, and the time is so short. We can proceed, of course, out of grim and angry desperation. But the tasks proceed more easily and productively with a measure of thankful-ness for life; it links us to our deeper powers and lets us rest in them. Many of us are braced, psychically and physically, against the signals of distress that continually barrage us in the news, on our streets, in our environment. As if to reduce their impact on us, we contract like a turtle into its shell. But we can choose to turn to the breath, the body, the senses—for they help us to relax and open to wider currents of knowing and feeling.

The great open secret of gratitude is that it is not dependent on external circumstance. It's like a setting or channel that we can switch to at any moment, no matter what's going on around us. It helps us connect to our basic right to be here, like the breath does. It's a stance of the soul. In systems theory, each part contains the whole. Gratitude is the kernel that can flower into everything we need to know.

Thankfulness loosens the grip of the industrial growth society by contradicting its predominant message: that we are insufficient and inadequate. The forces of late capitalism continually tell us that we need *more*—more stuff, more money, more approval, more comfort, more entertainment. The dissatisfaction it breeds is profound. It infects people with a compulsion to acquire that delivers them into the cruel, humiliating bondage of debt. So gratitude is liberating. It is subversive. It helps us realize that we are sufficient, and that realization frees us. Elders of indigenous cultures have retained this knowledge, and we can learn from their practices.

Learning from the Onondaga

Elders of the six-nation confederacy of the Haudenosaunee, also known as the Iroquois, have passed down through the ages the teachings of the Great Peacemaker. A thousand years ago, the nations had been warring tribes, caught in brutal cycles of attack, revenge, and retaliation, when the Great Peacemaker came across Lake Ontario in a stone canoe. Gradually his words and actions won them over, and they accepted the Great Law of Peace. They buried their weapons under the Peace Tree by Lake Onondaga, and formed councils for making wise choices together, and for self-governance. In the Haudenosaunee, historians recognize the oldest known participatory democracy, and point to the inspiration it provided to Benjamin Franklin, James Madison, and others in crafting the Constitution of the United States. That did not impede American settlers and soldiers from taking by force most of the Haudenosaunees' land and decimating their populations.

Eventually accorded "sovereign" status, the Haudenosaunee nations —all except for the Onondaga—proceeded in recent decades to sue state and federal governments for their ancestral lands, winning settlements in cash and license for casinos. All waited and wondered what legal action would be brought by the Onondaga Nation, whose name means Keepers of the Central Fire and whose ancestral land, vastly larger than the bit they now control, extends in a wide swath from Pennsylvania to Canada. But the Onondaga elders and clan mothers continued to deliberate year after year, seeking consensus on this issue that would shape the fate of their people for generations to come. Finally, in the spring of 2005, they made their legal move. In their land rights action, unlike that of any other indigenous group in America, they did not demand the return of any ancestral land or monetary compensation for it. They asked for one thing only: that it be cleaned up and restored to health for the sake of all who presently live on it, and for the sake of their children and children's children.

To state and federal power-holders, this was asking a lot. The land is heavily contaminated by industrial development, including big chemical processing plants and a number of neglected toxic waste sites. Onondaga Lake, on whose shores stood the sacred Peace Tree, is considered to be more polluted with heavy metals than any in the country. Within a year, at the urging of the governor of New York, the court dismissed the Onondaga action as invalid and too late.

On a bleak November afternoon, when the suit was still in process, I visited the Onondaga Nation—a big name for this scrap of land that looks like a postage stamp on maps of Central New York. I had come because I was moved by the integrity and vision of their land rights action, and now I saw how few material resources they possess to pursue it. In the community center, native counselors described outreach programs for mental health and self-esteem, bringing young people together from all the Haudenosaunee. To help with the expenses, other tribes had chipped in, but few contributions had been received from the richer ones.

They were eager for me to see the recently built school where young Onondagans, who choose not to go off the Nation to U.S.-run schools, can receive an education. A teacher named Freida, who was serving for a while as a clan mother, had waited after hours to show me around. The central atrium she led me into was hung about with shields of a dozen clans—turtle clan, bear clan, beaver—and on the floor illumined by the skylight was a large green turtle, beautifully wrought of inlaid wood. "Here is where we gather the students for our daily morning assembly," Freida explained. "We begin, of course, with the thanksgiving. Not the real, traditional form of it, because that takes over an hour and a half. We do it very short, just twenty minutes or so." Turning to gaze at her face, I sank down on a bench. She heard my silent request and sat down too. Raising her right hand in a circling gesture that spiraled downward as the fingers closed, she began. "Let us gather our minds as one mind and give thanks to our eldest Brother, the Sun, who rises each day to bring light so we can see each other's faces and warmth for the seeds to grow." On and on she continued, greeting and thanking the life-giving presences that bless and nourish us all. With each one—moon, waters, trees—that lovely gesture was repeated. "We gather our minds as one mind."

My eyes stayed riveted on her. What I was receiving through her words and gesture felt like an intravenous injection, right into my bloodstream. This, I knew, can teach us how to survive, when all possessions and comforts have been lost. When our honored place in the world is taken from us, this practice can hold us together in dignity and clear mind.

What Freida gave me is a staple of Haudenosaunee culture. The Mohawks have written down similar words, in an equally short form, so the rest of us can have it too.

The Mohawk Thanksgiving Prayer

The People

Today we have gathered and we see that the cycles of life continue. We have been given the duty to live in balance and harmony with each other and all living things. So now, we give greetings and thanks to each other as people.

Now our minds are one.

The Earth Mother

We are all thankful to our mother, the Earth, for she gives us all that we need for life. She supports our feet as we walk about upon her. It gives us joy that she continues to care for us as she has from the beginning of time. To our mother, we send greetings and thanks.

Now our minds are one.

The Waters

We give thanks to all the waters of the world for quenching our thirst and providing us with strength. Water is life. We know its power in many forms—waterfalls and rain, mists and streams, rivers and oceans. We send greetings and thanks to the spirit of water.

Now our minds are one.

The Fish

We turn our minds to all the fish life in the water. They were instructed to cleanse and purify the water. They also give themselves to us as food. We are grateful that we can still find pure water. So, we turn now to the fish and send our greetings and thanks.

Now our minds are one.

The Plants

Now we turn toward the vast fields of plant life. As far as the eye can see, the plants grow, working many wonders. They sustain many life forms. With our minds gathered together, we give thanks and look forward to seeing plant life for many generations to come.

Now our minds are one.

The Food Plants

With one mind, we turn to honor and thank all the food plants we harvest from the garden. Since the beginning of time, the grains, vegetables, beans, and berries have helped the people survive. Many other living things draw strength from them too. We gather all the plant foods together as one and send them a greeting of thanks.

Now our minds are one.

The Medicine Herbs

Now we turn to all the medicine herbs of the world. From the beginning they were instructed to take away sickness. They are always waiting and ready to heal us. We are happy there are still among us those special few who remember how to use these plants for healing. We send greetings and thanks to the medicines and to the keepers of the medicines.

Now our minds are one.

The Animals

We gather our minds together to send greetings and thanks to all the animal life in the world. They have many things to teach us as people. We are honored when they give up their lives so we may use their bodies as food for our people. We see them near our homes and in the deep forests. We are glad they are still here and we hope that it will always be so.

Now our minds are one

The Trees

We now turn our thoughts to the trees. The Earth has many families of trees who have their own instructions and uses. Some provide us with shelter and shade, others with fruit, beauty, and other useful things. Many people of the world use a tree as a symbol of peace and strength. We greet and thank the tree life.

Now our minds are one.

The Birds

We put our minds together as one and thank all the birds who move and fly about over our heads. The creator gave them beautiful songs. Each day they remind us to enjoy and appreciate life. The eagle was chosen to be their leader. To all the birds—from the smallest to the largest—we send our joyful greetings and thanks.

Now our minds are one.

The Four Winds

We are all thankful to the powers we know as the four winds. We hear their voices in the moving air as they refresh us and purify the air we breathe. They help us to bring the change of seasons. From the four directions they come, bringing us messages and giving us strength. We send our greetings and thanks to the four winds.

Now our minds are one.

Grandfather Thunder

Now we turn to the west where our grandfathers, the thunder beings, live. With lightning and thundering voices, they bring with them the water that renews life. We bring our minds together as one to send greetings and thanks to our grandfathers, the thunderers.

Now our minds are one.

Eldest Brother the Sun

We now send greetings and thanks to our eldest brother, the sun. Each day without fail he travels the sky from east to west, bringing the light of a new day. He is the source of all the fires of life. We send greetings and thanks to our brother, the sun.

Now our minds are one.

Grandmother Moon

We put our minds together to give thanks to our oldest grandmother, the moon, who lights the nighttime sky. She is the leader of women all over the world, and she governs the movement of the ocean tides. By her changing face we measure time, and it is the moon who watches over the arrival of children here on Earth. We send greetings and thanks to our grandmother, the moon.

Now our minds are one.

The Stars

We give thanks to the stars who are spread across the sky like jewelry. We see them in the night, helping the moon to light the darkness and bringing dew to the gardens and growing things. When we travel at night, they guide us home. With our minds gathered together as one, we send greetings and thanks to the stars.

Now our minds are one.

The Enlightened Teachers

We gather our minds to greet and thank the enlightened teachers who have come to help throughout the ages. When we forget how to live in harmony, they remind us of the way we were instructed to live as people. We send greetings and thanks to these caring teachers.
Now our minds are one.

The Creator

Now we turn our thoughts to the creator, or great spirit, and send greetings and thanks for all the gifts of creation. Everything we need to live a good life is here on this Mother Earth. For all the love that is still around us, we gather our minds together as one and send our choicest words of greetings and thanks to the creator.
Now our minds are one.

Closing Words

We have now arrived at the place where we end our words. Of all the things we have named, it was not our intention to leave anything out. If something was forgotten, we leave it to each individual to send such greetings and thanks in their own way.
Now our minds are one.

Love Letter to the Milky Way

Today, thanks to space telescopes and astrophysics, science affords us wider vistas into the world that birthed us. A new cosmology arises. With it comes a "universe story," such as narrated by Thomas Berry, Brian Swimme, Sister Miriam McGillis, and others. This narrative of our own developmental journey through time and space brings us new dimensions of awe and gratitude. Rap artist Drew Dellinger, founder of Poets for Global Justice, invites us into these dimensions, with his "Love Letter to the Milky Way."

I want to tell you about love
There are approximately 1 trillion galaxies
I want to tell you about
In the Milky Way there are about 100 billion stars
I want to tell you
Love is the breath of the cosmos

I want to write a love letter to the Milky Way
Everything is an expression of the galaxy
My 30 trillion cells
The four noble truths
The eightfold path
The five precepts
The seven energy centers of the body
Everything is the Milky Way
including my lover,
and every kiss
of every lover that's ever
lived

The deep sky
The ubiquity of spirit
The DNA of dreams
The interlocking patterns of the cosmic constellations

"Cosmos" and "justice" are synonymous with beauty
but parts of the Milky Way don't give off light
Sometimes it feels like I've got Ground Zero in my heart

The dark sun bleeds shadows
The dark sun leaves shadows on everything
The forecast calls for scattered to broken skies

If there wasn't so much love there wouldn't be so much pain
It's like love is the nervous system of the universe
bringing us joy and sorrow

I inherit the
voice of the Milky Way in my dreams
The entire galaxy revolves around a single drop of wine

Your skin
the texture of the cosmos
the religion beyond religion
I want to know you like the wind knows the canyons
or the rain knows the rivulets
Lightning is continuously striking in 100 places every moment
The universe spills through our dreams
The future belongs to the most compelling story
Even the word "love"
is not adequate to define
the fabric of
space-time

If we could sense everything at once
like Krishna entering history with all the memory of his past
incarnations
then I could tell you about love.

The Spiral

There are hard things to face in our world today, if we want to be of use. Gratitude, when it's real, offers no blinders. On the contrary, in the face of devastation and tragedy it can ground us, especially when we're scared. It can hold us steady for the work to be done.

The activist's inner journey appears to me like a spiral, interconnecting four successive stages or movements that feed into each other. These four are 1) opening to gratitude, 2) owning our pain for the world, 3) seeing with new eyes, and 4) going forth. The sequence repeats itself, as the spiral circles round, but ever in new ways. The spiral is fractal in nature: it can characterize a lifetime or a project, and it can also happen in a day or several times a day.

The spiral begins with gratitude, because that quiets the frantic mind and brings us back to source. It reconnects us with basic goodness and our personal power. It helps us to be more fully present to our world. That grounded presence provides the psychic space for acknowledging the pain we carry for our world.

In owning this pain, and daring to experience it, we learn that our capacity to "suffer with" is the true meaning of compassion. We begin to know the immensity of our heart-mind, and how it helps us to move beyond fear. What had isolated us in private anguish now opens outward and delivers us into wider reaches of our world as lover, world as self.

The truth of our inter-existence, made real to us by our pain for the world, helps us see with new eyes. It brings fresh understandings of who we are and how we are related to each other and the universe. We begin to comprehend our own power to change and heal. We strengthen by growing living connections with past and future generations, and our brother and sister species.

Then, ever again, we go forth into the action that calls us. With others whenever and wherever possible, we set a target, lay a plan, step out. We don't wait for a blueprint or fail-proof scheme; for each step will be our teacher, bringing new perspectives and opportunities. Even when we don't succeed in a given venture, we can be grateful for the chance we took and the lessons we learned. And the spiral begins again.

"Then all the work I put my hand to
widens from turn to turn."
                                —Rainer Maria Rilke

The Bestiary

7

Short-tailed albatross
    Whooping crane
        Gray wolf
            Woodland caribou
                Hawksbill sea turtle
                Rhinoceros

The lists of endangered species grow longer every year. With too many names to hold in our mind, how do we honor the passing of life? What funerals or farewells are appropriate?

Reed warbler
    Swallowtail butterfly
        Bighorn sheep
            Indian python
                Howler monkey
                    Sperm whale
                      Blue whale

Dive me deep, brother whale, in this time we have left. Deep in our mother ocean where I once swam, gilled, and finned. The salt from those early seas still runs in my tears. Tears aren't enough anymore. Give me a song, a song for a sadness too vast for my heart, for a rage too wild for my throat.

Giant sable antelope
    Wyoming toad
        Polar bear

Brown bear

Bactrian camel

Nile crocodile

Chinese alligator

Ooze me, alligator, in the mud whence I came. Belly me slow in the rich
primordial soup, cradle of our molecules. Let me wallow again, before
we drain your swamp and pave it over.

Gray bat

Ocelot

Pocket mouse

Sockeye salmon

Hawaiian goose

Audouin's seagull

Quick, lift off. Sweep me high over the coast and out, farther out. Don't
land here. Oil spills coat the beach, rocks, sea. I cannot spread my wings
glued with tar. Fly me from what we have done, fly me far.

Golden parakeet

West African ostrich

Florida panther

Galapagos penguin

Imperial pheasant

Mexican prairie dog

Hide me in a hedgerow, badger. Can't you find one? Dig me a tun-
nel through leaf-mold and roots, under the trees that once defined our
fields. My heart is bulldozed and plowed over. Burrow me a labyrinth
deeper than longing.

Thick-billed parrot

Blue pike

Snow leopard

Molokai thrush

California condor

Lotus blue butterfly

Crawl me out of here, caterpillar. Spin me a cocoon. Wind me to sleep
in a shroud of silk, where in patience my bones will dissolve. I'll wait as

long as all creation if only it will come again—and I take wing.
Atlantic Ridley turtle
> Coho salmon
>> Helmeted hornbill
>>> Marine otter
>>>> Humpback whale
>>>>> Steller sea lion
>>>>>> Monk seal

Swim me out beyond the ice floes, mama. Where are you? Boots squeeze
my ribs, clubs drum my fur, the white world goes black with the taste
of my blood.
Gibbon
> Sand gazelle
>> Swamp deer
>>> Musk deer
>>>> Cheetah
>>>>> Chinchilla
>>>>>> Asian elephant
>>>>>>> African elephant

Sway me slowly through the jungle. There still must be jungle some-
where. My heart drips with green secrets. Hose me down by the water-
hole; there is buckshot in my hide. Tell me old stories while you can
remember.
Desert tortoise
> Crested ibis
>> Hook-billed kite
>>> Mountain zebra
>>>> Tibetan antelope
>>>>> Andrew's frigatebird

In the time when his world, like ours, was ending, Noah had a list of
the animals, too. We picture him standing by the gangplank, calling
their names, checking them off on his scroll. Now we also are checking them off.

Ivory-billed woodpecker
    Indus river dolphin
        West Indian manatee
        Wood stork

We reenact Noah's ancient drama, but in reverse, like a film running backwards, the animals exiting.

Ferret
    Gorilla
        Tiger
        Wolf

Your tracks are growing fainter. Wait. Wait. This is a hard time. Don't leave us alone in a world we have wrecked.

Despair Work   8

The moon knows that if you deny the dark,
you make a mockery of the light.
—MARILYN KRYSL

A T THIS MOMENT ON Earth, we possess more technical prowess and knowledge than our ancestors could have dreamt of. Our telescopes let us see through time to the beginnings of the universe; our microscopes pry open the codes at the core of organic life; our satellites reveal global weather patterns and hidden behaviors of remote nations. Who, even a century ago, could have imagined such abundance of information and power?

At the same time we witness destruction of life in dimensions that confronted no previous generation in recorded history. Certainly our ancestors knew wars, plagues, and famine; entire civilizations foundered. But today it is not just a forest here and farmlands and fisheries there; today entire species are dying—and whole cultures and ecosystems on a global scale, even to the oxygen-producing plankton of our seas. What is in store for our children's children? What will be left for those who come after? Appalled by the questions themselves, we turn to immediate tasks and try to close our minds to nightmare scenarios of want and war in a wasted, contaminated world.

The Greatest Danger

When we are fearful, and the odds are running against us, it is easy to let the heart and mind go numb. Because the perils facing us are so pervasive, and yet often hard to see, this numbing touches us all. No one is unaffected by it. No one is immune to doubt, denial, or disbelief about the severity of our situation—and about our power to change it. Yet of all the dangers we face, from climate chaos to nuclear warfare, none is so great as the deadening of our response. The numbing of mind and heart is already upon us—in the diversions we create for ourselves as individuals and nations, in the fights we pick, the aims we pursue, the stuff we buy.

The very alarms that should rivet our attention and bond us in collective action tend to have the opposite effect. They make us want to pull down the blinds and busy ourselves with other things. We eat meat from factory-farmed animals and produce grown by agribusiness, knowing of the pesticides and hormones they contain, but preferring not to think they'll cause harm. We buy clothes without noticing where they are made, preferring not to think of the sweatshops they may have come from. We don't bother voting, or if we do, we vote for candidates we may not believe will address the real problems, hoping against all previous experience that they will suddenly awaken and act boldly to save us. Have we become callous, nihilistic? Have we ceased to care what happens to life on Earth?

Apatheia

It can look that way. Activists decry public apathy. The cause of our apathy, however, is not indifference. It stems from a fear of the despair that lurks beneath the tenor of life-as-usual. Sometimes it manifests in dreams of mass destruction, and is exorcised in the morning jog and shower or in the public fantasies of disaster movies. Because of social taboos against despair and because of fear of pain, it is rarely acknowledged or expressed directly. It is kept at bay. The suppression of despair, like that of any deep recurrent response, produces a partial numbing of the psyche. Expressions of anguish or outrage are muted, deadened as if a nerve had been cut.

The refusal to feel takes a heavy toll. It not only impoverishes our emotional and sensory life—flowers are dimmer and less fragrant, our loves less ecstatic—but also impedes our capacity to process and respond to information. The energy expended in pushing down despair is diverted from more creative uses, depleting the resilience and imagination needed for fresh visions and strategies. Fear of despair erects an invisible screen, filtering out anxiety-provoking data. In a world where organisms require feedback in order to adapt and survive, this is suicidal. Now, when we most need to measure the effects of our acts, our attention and curiosity slacken as if we are already preparing for the Big Sleep. Doggedly attending to business-as-usual, we're denying both our despair and our ability to cope with it.

So it's good to look at what apathy is, to understand it with respect and compassion. *Apatheia* is a Greek word that means, literally, non-suffering. Given its etymology, apathy is the inability or refusal to experience pain. What is the pain we feel—and desperately try not to feel—in this planet-time? It is of another order altogether than what the ancient Greeks could have known; it pertains not just to privations of wealth, health, reputation, or loved ones, but to losses so vast we can hardly name them. It is pain for the world.

Pain for the World

We cannot see or hear about what is happening to our world—be it job layoffs or homeless families, nearby toxic leaks or far-off famines, war or preparations for war—without emotion. Though we may rarely express them, feelings of fear, anger, and sorrow stir within us. Even the words—fear, anger, sorrow—are inadequate to convey the feelings that arise; for they connote emotions that humanity has known since time began. The feelings that arise now cannot be equated with ancient dreads of mortality. They arise from apprehensions of unprecedented collective suffering that is accruing to our own and other species, to unborn generations, and the living Earth itself.

Silence about these inner responses can obscure the fact that they are natural and universal. Like cells in a larger body, we sense when that body is traumatized. When it falters and sickens, we feel its pain, whether we pay attention to it or not. What we are dealing with here is akin to the original meaning of compassion—"suffering with." It is the distress we feel on behalf of the larger whole of which we are a part. No one is exempt from that pain, any more than one could exist alone and self-sufficient in empty space. It is as natural to us as the food and air we draw upon to fashion who we are. It is inseparable from the currents of matter, energy, and information that flow through us and sustain us as interconnected open systems. In the words of Franz Kafka:

> You can hold yourself back from the suffering of the world: this is something you are free to do, . . . but perhaps precisely this holding back is the only suffering you might be able to avoid.

Pain for the world is not only natural, it is a necessary component of our healing. As in all organisms, pain has a purpose: it is a warning signal, designed to trigger remedial action. It is not to be banished by injections of optimism or sermons on "positive thinking." It is to be named and validated as a healthy, normal human response to the situation we find ourselves in. Faced and experienced, its power can be used. As the frozen defenses of the psyche thaw, new energies and intelligence are released.

The problem lies not with our pain for the world, but in our repression of it. Our efforts to dodge or dull it surrender us to futility—or in systems terms, cut off the feedback loop and block appropriate response. Zen poet Thich Nhat Hanh was asked, "What do we most need to do to save our world?" His questioners expected him to identify the best strategies to pursue in social and environmental action, but Thich Nhat Hanh's answer was this: "What we most need to do is to hear within us the sounds of the Earth crying."

That is what my colleagues and I began to do in the late '70s: find ways we can help each other "hear the Earth crying within us." Drawing from systems theory and Buddhist teachings, we work mainly in groups, because the situation we face bears on us all. In sharing our innermost responses to the perils of our time, we rediscover our mutual belonging in the web of life, and the empowerment it brings to act on its behalf. "Despair work" was the name first attached to the theory and methods we developed, but over the years other names have followed, such as Deep Ecology Work and the Work That Reconnects. Although the group work soon expanded to include other stages and features, the owning and honoring of our pain for the world has remained an essential component. Rainforest activist John Seed, a facilitator of this work, explains it this way: "You discover that others aren't afraid of your pain for the world, and you witness theirs. Then you can dare to hope something for humanity and for what we can do together. When we unblock our despair, everything else follows—the respect and awe, the love."

Positive Disintegration

The prospect of uncovering our innermost feelings about what is happening to our world is daunting. How to confront what we scarcely dare to think? How to face such grief and fear and rage without going to pieces?

It is good to realize that falling apart is not such a bad thing. Indeed, it is as essential to evolutionary and psychological transformations as the cracking of outgrown shells. Polish psychiatrist Kazimierz Dabrowski calls it "positive disintegration." He sees it in every global development of humanity, especially during periods of accelerated change, and it functions to permit the emergence of "higher psychic structures and awareness." On the individual level, positive disintegration occurs when a person courageously confronts anomalies and contradictions of experience. It is like a dark night of the soul, a time of spiritual void and turbulence. But the anxieties and doubts are, Dabrowski maintains, "essentially healthy and creative." They are creative not only for the person but for society, because they permit new and original approaches to reality.

What "disintegrates" in periods of rapid transformation is not the self, but its defenses and ideas. We are not objects that can break. As open systems, we are, in the words of cybernetician Norbert Wiener, "but whirlpools in a river of everflowing water. We are not stuff that abides, but patterns that perpetuate themselves." We do not need to protect ourselves from change, for our very nature is change. Defensive self-protection, restricting vision and movement like a suit of armor, makes it harder to adapt. It not only reduces flexibility, but blocks the flow of information we need to survive. Our "going to pieces," however uncomfortable, can open us up to new perceptions, new data, and new responses.

Breaking the Spell

For Americans to get in touch with their pain for the world, a dark night of the soul may be hard to avoid. This is still the land of Dale Carnegie and Norman Vincent Peale, where an unflagging optimism is taken as the means and measure of success. As commercials for products and campaigns of politicians attest, the healthy and admirable person smiles a lot. The feelings of depression, loneliness, and anxiety, to which this thinking animal has always been heir, carry here an added burden: one feels bad about feeling bad. One can even feel guilty about it. In a country built on utopian expectations, failure to hope can seem downright un-American.

In our culture despair is feared and resisted because it represents a loss of control. Our culture dodges it by demanding instant solutions when problems are raised. My political science colleagues in France ridiculed this trait of the American personality. "You people prescribe before you finish the diagnosis," they would say. "Let the difficulties reveal themselves first before rushing for a ready-made solution or else you will not understand them." To do this would require that one view a stressful situation without the psychic security of knowing if and how it can be solved—in other words, a readiness to suffer a little.

"Don't bring me a problem unless you have a solution," Lyndon B. Johnson is quoted as saying during the Vietnam War. That injunction rings like the words my mother said to me as a child, "If you can't say something nice, don't say anything at all."

This cultural habit casts a kind of spell, obscuring perceptions and fostering a dangerous innocence of the real world. The current president and administration deepen this spell. Corporate monopolization of the media and the wreckage of our public school system keep a large portion of Americans ignorant of the forces threatening their own future, while the state of the economy robs them of time and energy to respond to larger issues. With job losses from corporate mergers and the decimation of health and welfare programs, life narrows down to immediate survival needs—and there is little time to learn about the fate of the world, or let it sink in. If a free hour is left at the end of the day, it's easier to zone out in front of the television and the packaged fantasies of the industrial growth society.

Even if we have inklings of apocalypse, the American trance functions to discourage our feelings of despair and, if they persist, to reduce them to personal pathologies. Though we may respect our own cognitive reading of the signs, the spell we are under often leads us to imagine that it is we, not the society, who are going insane. Such internalizing is helped along by those psychotherapists who still have difficulty crediting the notion that concerns for the general welfare might be acute enough to cause distress. Assuming that all our drives are ego-centered, they tend to reduce this distress to a manifestation of private neurosis. In my own case, anguish over destruction of wilderness was diagnosed as fear of my own libido, which the bulldozers were taken to symbolize, and my painful preoccupation with U.S. bombings of Vietnam was interpreted as an unwholesome hangover of Puritan guilt. I probably would have been medicated with antidepressants if they had been as widely prescribed back then as they are now.

Years ago, a Jungian psychologist, after taking part in a "despair and empowerment" workshop, made an observation I'll never forget. Noting how people's sharing of their pain for the world had led to an upwelling of energy and high-spirited plans for action, he likened the experience to the tale of Sleeping Beauty. The princess had been asleep for a hundred years and nothing could wake her till the prince made his way through the brambles and thorns surrounding her castle. It was his kiss that broke the spell. "This despair work," he said, "is like that kiss. It delivers us from the trance."

Truth-Telling

What broke the spell was not an informative lecture. I had delivered no diagnosis of the world's ills or prescriptions for action. The workshop offered a more distinctive and rare opportunity: the chance to hear from others, and especially from oneself. The one we most need to listen to, I believe, is the person inside, for only she or he can break the censorship we impose upon ourselves.

Despair work involves nothing more mysterious than telling the truth about what we see and know and feel is happening to our world. This should be as simple as telling someone the time of day, if it were not for all that isolates us from each other and befuddles us with self-doubt. When corporate-controlled media keep the public in the dark, and power-holders manipulate events to create a climate of fear and obedience, truth-telling is like oxygen.

When we help each other to tell the truth, and open to the feelings that go with it, we validate our common experience and forge bonds of solidarity. The practice of intentional truth sharing is happening worldwide. Inspired by the Truth and Reconciliation Commission in South Africa, the establishment of truth commissions has spread to twenty other countries, such as El Salvador, Sierra Leone, and East Timor. To attest publicly to one's own role in a tragedy, and to the trauma one has suffered, requires courage, and strengthens it in turn. These commissions are a marvel of our time, teaching us ways to mend what has been broken and restore the integrity of victims and perpetrators alike.

In the U.S., a Truth-Telling Project has been founded by Daniel Ellsberg, the man who released the Pentagon Papers, exposing the official lies behind the Vietnam War. Encouraging "whistle-blowing in the national interest, it urges current and recently retired government officials to reveal the truth to Congress and the public about governmental wrongdoing, lies, and cover-up. It aims to change the norms and practices that sustain the cult of secrecy, and to de-legitimize silence that costs lives." People are emerging to speak out, like insider John Perkins, whose book *Confessions of an Economic Hit Man* reveals far-reaching fraud within the World Bank, International Monetary Fund, and other institutions controlling flows of global wealth. It was on the New York Times Bestseller list for many weeks. We, as a people, are hungry for truth.

The use of ritual for truth-telling can be powerful, as I've discovered in my work with groups. Ritual can provide a simple, safe, whole-group structure for expressing and honoring our pain for the world and for finding the authority it can bring. One such form, the Truth Mandala, has proved so effective in the spontaneity and respect it engenders, that it has spread fast and far, as participants take it out to their own communities and places of work. Instructions for leading it are given in my book *Coming Back to Life,* but a few words here may convey its character.

We sit in a circle, creating a containment vessel for receiving and holding the truth. The space we enclose is divided into four quadrants, and in each quadrant is placed an object: a stone, a thick stick, a handful of dead leaves, an empty bowl. The dead leaves symbolize sorrow, the stone stands for fear, the stick is our anger, and the empty bowl represents our emptiness, confusion, and need. After dedicating the ritual to the healing of our world, we are free to rise and enter the mandala one at a time, as we feel moved. Taking in our hands the object of our choice, we "let it speak through us," as we say, giving voice to how we experience it in our own life. Sometimes the "speaking" is through silence or tears, a prayer or a song. After each utterance, the group responds in simple acknowledgment: "We hear you."

At the start and again at the end of the ritual, the fuller meaning of the symbols is told. Each object holds a deeper import, like a coin with two sides. Our sorrow is the other face of love, for we only mourn what we deeply care for. The courage to speak our fear is evidence of our trust; our anger reveals our passion for justice; and the emptiness creates space for the new to arise.

Thus do we realize ever again that the simple eloquence of telling the truth liberates us to find insight, solidarity, and courage to act, despite rapidly worsening conditions. When we face the darkness of our time, openly and together, we tap deep reserves of strength within us. Many of us fear that confrontation with despair will bring loneliness and isolation, but—on the contrary—in the letting go of old defenses, truer community is found. In the synergy of sharing comes power. In community, we learn to trust our inner responses to our world—and find our power.

Beyond Urgency

> There are those who would set fire to the world.
> We are in danger.
> There is time only to move slowly.
> There is no time not to love.
>
> —Deena Metzger

Panic and paralysis are twins; both are born from refusal to wait. *Kshanti,* one of the paramitas or "perfections" of the bodhisattva, calls us to patience. It is essential to perseverance for the long haul. To accept and abide in the not-knowing of the moment is the antidote to burnout and helps us sustain our work. Pablo Neruda invites us to develop a "burning patience" in order to bring the light of justice and dignity into our turbulent time.

"The ability to wait is central to hope," writes William Lynch. Waiting does not mean inaction, but staying in touch with our pain and confusion as we act, not banishing them to grab for sedatives, ideologies, or final solutions. It is, as a student of mine quoted, "staying in the dark until the darkness becomes full and clear." The caterpillar, after a life of voracious consumption, wraps itself in a chrysalis. In the darkness of its cocoon, metamorphosis takes place as imaginal cells weave structures that, when the time is ripe, emerge as the miracle of butterfly.

Jacob Needleman suggests that part of the great danger in this time of crisis is that we may short-circuit despair, and thereby lose the revelations which can open to us.

> For there is nothing to guarantee that we will be able to remain long enough or deeply enough in front of the unknown, a psychological state which the traditional paths have always recognized as sacred. In that fleeting state between dreams, which is called "despair" in some Western teachings and "self-questioning" in Eastern traditions, a man is said to be able to receive the truth, both about nature and his own possible role in the universal order.

When I first confronted my own despair, I was haunted by the question, "What do you substitute for hope?" I had always assumed that a sanguine confidence in the future was as essential as air to breathe. Without it, I had thought, one would collapse into apathy and nihilism. It puzzled me that, after owning my despair, the energy I devoted to peace and environmental causes did not lessen, but increased.

One day I talked with Jim Douglass, the theologian and writer who had left his university post to resist nuclear weapons, and was jailed repeatedly for civil disobedience. He had said he believed we had five years left before it was too late to avert the use of our nuclear arsenal in a first strike strategy. I reflected on the implications of that remark and watched his face, as he squinted in the sun with an air of presence and serenity I could not fathom. "What do you substitute for hope?" I asked. He looked at me and smiled. "Possibilities," he said. "Possibilities . . . you can't predict, just make space for them. There are so many." That, too, is waiting, active waiting—moving out on the fog-bound trail, though you cannot see the way ahead.

Let This Darkness Be a Bell Tower

During the early months of the U.S. invasion of Iraq in 2003, I was working on a translation of Rilke's *Sonnets to Orpheus*. The poet's befriending of the dark, and the strength he drew from it, has always inspired me. But right then, as I struggled to come to terms with the brutal arrogance and perfidy of my own government, and the immense suffering in store, his words were like medicine. One poem in particular, the last sonnet, brought a kind of sanity and solace. My co-translator, Anita Barrows, and I took refuge in it. Our manner of working together is dialogical, reading the lines aloud over and over, back and forth—German-English-German—to find phrases that best capture their meaning and tone. With Sonnet II/29 we have kept on doing that, letting the words become part of us. Phrases like "let this darkness be a bell tower and you the bell," and "what batters you becomes your strength" will probably resonate inside us till we die. I think the sonnet as a whole sums up what I wanted to say in this chapter, and perhaps even the entire book:

> Quiet friend who has come so far,
> feel how your breathing makes more space around you.
> Let this darkness be a bell tower
> and you the bell. As you ring,
>
> what batters you becomes your strength.
> Move back and forth into the change.
> What is it like, such intensity of pain?
> If the drink is bitter, turn yourself to wine.
>
> In this uncontainable night,
> be the mystery at the crossroads of your senses,
> the meaning discovered there.
>
> And if the world has ceased to hear you,
> say to the silent earth: I flow.
> To the rushing water, speak: I am.

FAITH, POWER, AND ECOLOGY 9

"If we surrendered to earth's intelligence
we could rise up rooted, like trees."
—RAINER MARIA RILKE

T HESE WORDS TAKE ME back to a morning in Great Britain. I was standing for an hour in the sweet, gentle, English drizzle. In a large meadow were about forty men and women; three of them held toddlers. We stood in a circle and in the center rose two ancient, sacred stones. We had come there at the close of a five-day workshop on ecology, and our band included activists from all over the island—social workers, civil servants, artisans, teachers, homemakers—drawn together by a common concern for the fate of our planet.

In the presence of the standing stones, thousands of years old, we seemed to find ourselves in two dimensions of time simultaneously. One was vast and immeasurable. As we reached back to the ancient Earth wisdom of the culture that erected the stones, we sensed the long, long journey of life unfolding on this planet. At the same time, we were acutely aware of this particular historical moment when forces that our culture has unleashed are threatening to destroy our world.

We were people with different cultural and religious backgrounds, yet, despite the differing tradition systems to which we belonged, the prayers and affirmations that spontaneously arose in that circle expressed a common faith and fueled a common hope. Those words bespoke a shared commitment to engage in actions and changes in

lifestyle on behalf of our Earth and its beings. They expressed a bond-
ing to this Earth, going beyond feeling sorry for the planet or scared
for ourselves. They were an affirmation of relationship—relationship
that can be spiritually as well as physically sustaining, a relationship
that can empower.

Faith is an elusive and questionable commodity in these days of
a dying culture. Where do you find it? If you've lost a faith, can you
invent one? Which faith to choose? Some of us have retained a faith in
a just creator God or in a lawful, benevolent order to the universe. But
some of us find it hard, even obscene, to believe in an abiding provi-
dence in a world of such absurdity that, in the face of unimaginable
suffering, most of our wealth and wits are devoted to preparing a final
holocaust. And we don't need nuclear bombs for that holocaust; it is
going on right now in the demolition of the great rain forests and the
toxic contamination of our seas, soil, and air.

In a world like this, what can faith mean? The very notion can
appear distasteful, especially when we see faith widely used as an
excuse for denial and inaction. "God won't let it happen." Or even,
in some circles today, "It is God's will"—a fearful assertion when it
refers to nuclear war as the final and holy battle to exterminate the
wicked. The radical uncertainties of our time breed fundamentalism,
self-righteousness, and deep divisions. These uncertainties can turn
patriotism into xenophobia, incite fear and hatred of dissenters and
foreigners, and feed the engines of war.

Another option opens, however, that can lead to a more profound
and authentic form of faith. We can turn from the search for personal
salvation or some metaphysical haven, and look instead to our actual
experience. When we simply attend to what we see, feel, and know is
happening to our world, we find authenticity. Going down into a darkness where there appears to be no faith, we can make three important
discoveries. I see them as redeeming discoveries that can ground us in
our ecology and serve as our faith. These three are: (1) the discovery
of what we know and feel, (2) the discovery of what we are, and (3) the
discovery of what can happen through us or, one might say, grace.

Discovering What We Know and Feel

To discover what we know and feel is not as easy as it sounds, because a great deal of effort in contemporary society is devoted to keeping us from being honest. Entire industries are focused on persuading us that we are happy, or on the verge of being happy as soon as we buy this toothpaste or that automobile. It is not in the self-perceived interest of multinational corporations, or the government and the media that serve them, for us to stop and become aware of our profound anguish with the way things are.

None of us, in our hearts, is free of sorrow for the suffering of other beings. None of us is indifferent to the dangers that threaten our planet's people, or free of fear for the generations to come. Yet it is not easy to give credence to this anguish in a culture that enjoins us to "keep smiling," "be sociable," "go shopping."

Blocking of our natural responses to actual or impending disaster is part of the disease of our time, explains Robert Jay Lifton, the psychiatrist who pioneered the study of the psychological effects of nuclear bombing. The refusal to acknowledge these responses, or even feel them, produces a profound and dangerous splitting. It divorces our mental calculations from our intuitive, emotional, and biological sense. That split allows us passively to acquiesce in the preparations for our own demise.

As scholar-activist Joel Kovel asserts, we are made subservient and passive by "the state of nuclear terror." This terror is not the fear of nuclear weapons or other forms of mass annihilation so much as our fear of experiencing the fear. We are afraid that we might break apart or get stuck in despair if we open our eyes to the horrors. So the messages we tend to hear and to give are: "Don't talk to me about acid rain, or the arms race. There is nothing I can do about it. I have a family to support, a job to keep. If I were to take it all in and allow myself to think about it and *feel it*, I wouldn't be able to function."

The first discovery, opening to what we know and feel, takes courage. Like Gandhi's *satyagraha*, it involves "truth-force." People are not going to find their truth-force or inner authority in listening to the experts, but in listening to themselves. Every one of us is an expert on what it is like to live on an endangered planet. To affirm that expertise and counter habits of repression, a form of group work has evolved. In the Work That Reconnects, people come together to find their own inner authority. Without mincing words, without apology, embarrassment, or fear of causing distress, they simply tell the truth about their experience of this world. A boy talks about the dead fish in a stream he loves; a young couple wonders about the Strontium 90 in the bones of their children. To quote Justin Kenrick, a colleague in this work:

> We need permission in our minds and hearts and guts to accept that we are destroying the Earth and to feel the reality of who we are in that context; isolated, desperate, and powerless individuals, defeated by our old patterns of behavior before we have even begun to try to heal our lives and the Earth. Only then can we give ourselves permission to feel the power our culture denies us, to regain our intuitive sense of everything being in relation rather than in opposition, to regain our intuitive sense of the deep miraculous pattern to life that opens to us as we accept it.

In acknowledging our pain for the world, we return once more to the original meaning of *compassion:* "to suffer with." Suffering with our world, we are drawn into the cauldron of compassion. It is there. It awaits us; and as Kenrick's words suggest, it can reconnect us with our power.

Discovering What We Are

Acknowledging the depths and reaches of our own inner experience, we come to the second discovery: the discovery of what we are. We are experiencers of compassion. Buddhism has a term for that kind of being—it is "bodhisattva." The bodhisattva, the Buddhist model for heroic behavior, knows there is no such thing as private salvation. She or he does not hold aloof from this suffering world or try to escape from it, but returns again and again to work on behalf of all beings. For the bodhisattva knows that there is no healing without connection.

The sutras, or scriptures, tell us that we are all bodhisattvas, and our fundamental interconnections are portrayed in the beautiful image of the Jeweled Net of Indra. It is similar to the holographic model of the universe we find emerging from contemporary science. In the cosmic canopy of Indra's Net, each of us is a multifaceted jewel at each node of the net. Every jewel reflects all the others and sees the others reflecting back. That is what we find when we hear the sounds of the Earth crying within us. The tears that come are not ours alone: they are the tears of an Iraqi mother looking for her children in the rubble; they are the tears of a Navajo uranium miner learning that he is dying of cancer. We find we are interwoven threads in the intricate tapestry of life, its deep ecology.

What happens for us then is what every major religion has sought to offer—a shift in identification, a shift from the isolated "I" to a vaster sense of what we are. This is understandable not only as a spiritual experience, but also, in scientific terms, as an evolutionary development. As living forms evolve on this planet, we move not only in the direction of diversification, but toward integration as well. These two movements complement and enhance each other. Open systems self-organize and integrate by virtue of their differentiation, and they differentiate by virtue of their interactions. As we evolved we progressively shed our shells, our armor, our separate encasements; we grew soft, sensitive, vulnerable protuberances—eyes, lips, fingertips—to better connect and receive information, to better interweave our discoveries. If we are all bodhisattvas, it is because that thrust to connect, that capacity to integrate with and through each other, is our true nature.

In his book *Ecology and Man,* Paul Shepard writes: "We are hidden from ourselves by patterns of perception. Our thought forms, our language, encourage us to see ourselves or a plant or an animal as an isolated sac, a thing, a contained self, whereas the epidermis of the skin is ecologically like a pond surface or a forest soil, not a shell so much as a delicate interpenetration." Paul Shepard is calling us to a faith in our very biology. He goes on to say, "Affirmation of its own organic essence will be the ultimate test of the human mind."

We begin to see that a shift of identification can release us not only from the prison cell of ego, but also from the tight compartment of a solely human perspective. As John Seed, founder of the Rainforest Information Centre in Australia, points out, it takes us "beyond anthropocentrism." In his essay by that title, he says that anthropocentrism or human chauvinism is similar to sexism, but substitute "human race" for man and "all other species" for woman. And he says,

> When humans investigate and see through their layers of anthropocentric self-cherishing, a most profound change in consciousness begins to take place. Alienation subsides. The human is no longer an outsider apart. Your humanness is then recognized as being merely the most recent stage of your existence; as you stop identifying exclusively with this chapter, you start to get in touch with yourself as vertebrate, as mammal, as species only recently emerged from the rainforest. As the fog of amnesia disperses, there is a transformation in your relationship to other species and in your commitment to them . . . The thousands of years of imagined separation are over and we can begin to recall our true nature; that is, the change is a spiritual one—thinking like a mountain, sometimes referred to as deep ecology. As your memory improves . . . there is an identification with all life . . . Remember our childhood as rocks, as lava? Rocks contain the potentiality to weave themselves into such stuff as this. We are the rocks dancing.

Being Acted Through

That leads us to the third discovery we can make in our ecological Pilgrim's Progress. It is the discovery of what can happen through us. If we are the rocks dancing, then that which evolved us from those

rocks carries us forward now and sustains us in our work for the con-
tinuance of life.

When I admired a nurse for her strength and devotion in keeping
long hours in the children's ward, she shrugged off my compliment as
if it were entirely misplaced. "It's not *my* strength, you know. I get it
from the life in *them,*" she said, nodding at the rows of cots and cribs.
"They give me what I need to keep going." Whether tending a garden
or cooking in a soup kitchen, there is the sense of being sustained
by something beyond one's own individual power, of being acted
"through." It is close to the religious concept of grace, but distinct
from the traditional Western understanding of grace, as it does not
require belief in God or a supernatural agency. One simply finds oneself empowered to act on behalf of other beings—or on behalf of the
larger whole—and the empowerment itself seems to come "through"
that or those for whose sake one acts. In the ecological context, this
phenomenon can be understood as synergy. It helps us re-conceptual-
ize our very notion of what power is.

From the ecological perspective, all open systems—be they cells or
organisms, cedars or swamps—are seen to be self-organizing. They
don't require any external or superior agency to regulate them, any
more than your liver or an apple tree needs to be told how to function.
In other words, order is implicit in life; it is integral to life processes.
This contrasts with the hierarchical worldview our culture held for
centuries, where mind is set above nature and where order is assumed
to be something imposed from above on otherwise random, material
stuff. We have tended to define power in the same way, seeing it as
imposed from above. So we have equated power with domination,
with one thing exerting its will over another. It becomes a zero-sum or
win-lose game, where to be powerful means to resist the demands or
influences of another, and strong defenses are necessary to maintain
one's advantage.

In falling into this way of thinking, we lost sight of the fact that
this is not the way nature works. Living systems evolve in complexity,
flexibility, and intelligence through interaction with each other. These

interactions require openness and vulnerability in order to process the flow-through of energy and information. They bring into play new responses and new possibilities not previously present, increasing the capacity to effect change. This interdependent release of fresh potential is called synergy. It is like grace, because it brings an increase of power beyond one's own capacity as a separate entity.

The Power to Connect

I see the operation of this kind of grace everywhere I go. I see it, for example, in the movement of popular assemblies that sprung up spontaneously in Argentina following the government's default on its International Monetary Fund loans and the ensuing collapse of the economy. When bank accounts were frozen, over a million people took part in the "tin pot insurrection," coming onto the streets or hanging out of windows to bang on cooking pots, saucepans, or tea kettles to declare their resistance. The president resigned that night and four more governments fell in the following weeks. From the rubble of the neo-liberal model rose the cries of *Ya Basta!* Enough! Some three hundred factories and enterprises were taken over by their own workers. People from all classes and walks of life came together in parks, churches, or on street corners to share ideas, plan for collectively operated schools and hospitals, and take back control of their lives.

I see grace in the movement to shut down the infamous School of the Americas in Fort Benning, Georgia where the U.S. government has trained thousands of military and paramilitary personnel, as well as a good number of dictators throughout Latin America in the arts of terror, torture, and assassination. Graduates of the school are responsible for some of the grossest human rights abuses and civilian massacres in Latin America. At annual protests now spanning over twenty years, rapidly mounting numbers of protesters—clergy, students, veterans, plain citizens from all walks of life—have come to stand at the gates in solidarity with the peoples of Latin America, and to call for the school's closure. The streets are filled with grandmothers holding giant puppets that represent liberation struggles or children silently carrying white crosses in a funeral procession. Every year, hundreds of people "cross the line," and face up to six months in federal prison for their dissent. By risking action together, action that make them more vulnerable and more connected, their power has increased.

There are countless such innovative grassroots actions; they do not make headlines, but taken all together, they amount to an unprecedented explosion of people who are quietly putting concern for our common fate ahead of personal profit or pleasure. I see it in the growing number of citizens who are refusing to pay taxes for weapons of war; I see it in the thousands of Americans who travel to Palestine to stand in front of bulldozers or accompany ambulances in the streets. I see it in the alliances between Amazonian peoples and eco-warriors from around the world, coming together to defend the land from corporate oil drilling and pipelines. I see it among the American soldiers who are facing court martial and jail sentences for their refusal to serve and for publicly declaring the illegality of their nation's war and occupation of Iraq. I see it among the many other veterans across the United States who rally to support them. As they do this, they expand our understanding of patriotism, demonstrating that love for one's country does not have to exclude the other beings of our planet.

These people demonstrate what can happen through us when we break free of the old hierarchical notions of power. They show that grace happens when we act with others on behalf of our world.

Roots of Power

What can we do to nourish these efforts and strengthen the bodhisattva in ourselves? Two ways that I know are through community and practice. The liberation struggles in Latin America and the Philippines have demonstrated the efficacy of spiritually-based communities for nonviolent action. These tough networks of trust arise on the neighborhood level, as people strive together to understand, in their own terms and for their own situation, what they need to do to live without fear and injustice. These groups can be just ordinary people meeting regularly in a discipline of honest searching and mutual commitment.

In our own society, too, such communities have been arising in the form of local support and action groups. Here neighbors or coworkers, parents or professionals organize and meet regularly to support each other in action—be it in responding to the poisons leaching from a nearby dump or to the need for a peace curriculum in the local school. Those of us who participate in such "base communities" know that they enhance both personal integrity and our belief in what is possible.

In addition to such external support, we need, in this time of great challenge, the internal support of personal practice. I mean practice in the spiritual sense of fortifying the mind and schooling its attitudes. Because for generations we have been conditioned by the mechanistic, anthropocentric assumptions of our mainstream culture, intellectual assent to an ecological vision of life is not enough to change our perceptions and behaviors. The heart-mind needs to be trained to decondition our responses that are based on narrow notions of the self. The imagination needs to be schooled in order to experience our inter-existence with all beings in the web of life.

Spiritual exercises for cultivating reverence for life arise now out of many traditions and are welcomed by people regardless of their religious affiliation. I have found adaptations from Buddhist practices particularly helpful because they are grounded in the recognition of the dependent co-arising or deep ecology of all things. Similarly, Native American prayers and ritual forms, evoking our innate capacity to love and respect our Earth, are increasingly adapted and included in gatherings for work and worship. This is a prayer from the Laguna Pueblo people:

> I add my breath to your breath
> that our days may be long on the Earth,
> that the days of our people may be long,
> that we shall be as one person,
> that we may finish our road together.

THREE LESSONS IN COMPASSION   1O

I still arrive, in order to laugh and cry,
to fear and to hope.
The rhythm of my heart is the birth and death
of all that is alive.
—THICH NHAT HANH

I THOUGHT I KNEW what compassion was—it is a familiar concept, common to all religions. But in that first summer I spent
with the Tibetans, it appeared in dimensions new to my experience. I wasn't a student of Buddhism then, when I lived in India with
my husband and children, and first encountered Tibetan refugees in
the foothills of the Himalayas. Nor was it, I thought, interest in the
Dharma that drew me back to them the following summer—back to
that ragtag collection of monks and lamas and laypeople who, with
their leader Khamtrul Rinpoche, had come out from Kham in eastern
Tibet. I simply wanted to be around them. I felt a kind of wild gladness in their company, and imagined I could be of some use.

Despite their colorful, stirring ceremonies, they were in difficult
straits. Prey to diseases unknown in Tibet, they were living hand to
mouth, crowded into rented, derelict bungalows in the hill station of
Dalhousie. With no remunerative livelihood or land of their own, they
were at risk of being separated from each other and shipped off by
Indian government authorities to different work projects, road gangs,
camps, schools, orphanages, and other institutions being set up for

the thousands of refugees from Chinese repression in Tibet. So, along with an American Peace Corps volunteer, I worked to help them develop an economic base that would enable them to stay together as a community. When my children were free from school in Delhi, we moved up to Dalhousie for the summer.

Our goal was to help the refugees draw on their rich artistic heritage to produce crafts for sale, and to set up a cooperative marketing scheme. In the process friendships took root that would change my life.

It was clear that the Rinpoches, the incarnate lamas of the community, were great masters of Tibetan Buddhism, but I did not ask for teachings. Given the conditions with which they were coping, and the demands on their attention and health, that seemed presumptuous. I wanted to ease their burdens, not add to them. The precious hours when we were free to be together were devoted to concocting plans for the community, applying for government rations, or choosing wools, dyes, and designs for carpet production. Walking between my rented cottage with four children above Dalhousie's upper circle road and the Khampa community on a lower ridge a mile below, there was not time anyway for reading scriptures or learning meditation. But the teachings came anyway. They came in simple, unexpected ways. Three incidents live vividly in my memory.

One day, after my morning time with the children, I was walking down the mountain to meet with my Khampa friends. Before heading off, I had accompanied my oldest, eleven-year-old son to an impromptu Dharma class for Westerners at a school for young Tibetan lamas. The English-speaking nun in charge was teaching and she said, "So countless are all sentient beings, and so many their births throughout time, that each at some point was your mother." She then explained a practice for developing compassion: it consisted of viewing each person as your mother in a former life.

I played with the idea as I walked on down the mountain, following a narrow, winding road between cedars and rhododendron trees. The astronomical number of lifetimes that the nun's words evoked boggled my mind—yet the intent of this quaint practice, for all of its far-fetched fantasy, was touching. What a pity, I thought, that this was not a practice I could use, since reincarnation hardly featured as part of my worldview. Then I paused on the path as the figure of a laborer approached.

Load-bearing laborers were a familiar sight on the roads of Dalhousie, and the most heavily laden of all were those who struggled up the mountain with mammoth logs on their backs. They were low-caste mountain folk whose bent, gaunt forms were dwarfed by their burdens, many meters long. I had become accustomed to the sight of them, and accustomed as well to the sense of consternation that it triggered in me. I would usually look away in discomfort, and pass by with internally muttered judgments about the kind of social and economic system that so exploited its own population.

This afternoon I stood stock still. I watched the slight, bandy-legged figure move slowly uphill towards me, negotiating its burden—which looked like the trunk of a cedar—around the bend. Backing up to prop the rear of the log against the bank, and ease the weight of it, the laborer paused to catch his breath. "Namaste," I said softly, and stepped hesitantly toward him.

I wanted to see his face. But he was still strapped under his log, and I would have had to crouch down under it to look up at his features— which I ached now to see. What face did she now wear, this dear one who had long ago mothered me? My heart trembled with gladness and distress. I wanted to touch that dark, half-glimpsed cheek, and meet those lidded eyes bent to the ground. I wanted to undo and rearrange the straps that I might share his burden up the mountain. Whether out of respect or embarrassment, I did not do that. I simply stood five feet away and drank in every feature of that form—the grizzled chin, the rag turban, the gnarled hands grasping the forward overhang of log.

The customary comments of my internal social scientist evaporated. What appeared now before me was not an oppressed class or an indictment of an economic system, so much as a distinct, irreplaceable, and incomparably precious being. My mother. My child. A thousand questions rose urgently in my mind. Where was he headed?

When would he reach home? Would there be loved ones to greet him and a good meal to eat? Was there rest in store, and songs, and embraces?

When the man heaved the log off the bank to balance its weight on his back again and proceed uphill, I headed on down the mountain path. I had done nothing to change his life, or betray my discovery of our relationship. But the Dalhousie mountainside shone in a different light; the furnishings of my mind had been rearranged, my heart broken open. How odd, I thought, that I did not need to believe in reincarnation for that to happen.

The second incident occurred soon after, on a similar summer Dalhousie afternoon. It was one of the many tea times with Khamtrul Rinpoche, the head of the refugee community from Kham, and two of his younger tulkus or incarnate lamas, when we were devising plans for their craft production center. As usual, Khamtrul Rinpoche had a stretched canvas propped at his side on which, with his customary, affable equanimity, he would be painting as we drank our tea and talked. His great round face exuded a serene confidence that our deliberations would bear fruit, just as the Buddha forms on his canvas would take form under the fine sable brush in his hands.

I, as usual, was seized by urgency to push through plans for the craft cooperative and requests for grants. I could not know then that this work would eventuate in the monastic settlement of Tashi Jong, where in a few years, the 400-member community of Khampa monks and laypeople would sink their roots in exile.

On this particular afternoon a fly fell into my tea. This was, of course, a minor occurrence. After a year in India I considered myself to be unperturbed by insects, be they ants in the sugar bin, spiders in the cupboard, and even scorpions in my shoes in the morning. Still, as I lifted my cup, I must have registered, by my facial expression or a small grunt, the presence of the fly. Choegyal Rinpoche, the eighteen-year-old tulku who was already becoming my friend for life, leaned forward in sympathy and consternation. "What is the matter?"

"Oh, nothing," I said. "It's nothing—just a fly in my tea." I laughed lightly to convey my acceptance and composure. I did not want him to suppose that mere insects were a problem for me; after all, I was an experienced traveler in India, relatively free of Western phobias and attachments to modern sanitation.

Choegyal crooned softly, in apparent commiseration with my plight, "Oh, oh, a fly in the tea." "It's no problem," I reiterated, smiling at him reassuringly. But he continued to focus great concern on my cup. Rising from his chair, he leaned over and inserted his finger into my tea. With great care he lifted out the offending fly—and then exited from the room. The conversation at the table resumed. I was eager to obtain Khamtrul Rinpoche's agreement on plans to secure the high-altitude wool he desired for the carpet production.

When Choegyal Rinpoche reentered the cottage he was beaming. "He is going to be all right," he told me quietly. He explained how he had placed the fly on the leaf of a branch by the door, where his wings could dry. And the fly was still alive, because he began fanning his wings, and we could confidently expect him to take flight soon . . .

That is what I remember of that afternoon—not the agreements we reached or plans we devised, but Choegyal's report that the fly would live. And I recall, too, the laughter in my heart. I could not, truth to tell, share Choegyal's dimensions of compassion, but the pleasure in his face revealed how much I was missing by not extending my self-concern to *all* beings, even to flies. The very notion that it was possible gave me boundless delight.

My third lesson that summer also occurred casually, in passing. In order to help the Tibetans I wanted to tell their story to the world— a story I was just beginning to discover. I had stunning photos of the Tibetans in exile, of their faces and crafts, and the majestic lama dances of their lineage. I envisaged an illustrated article for a popular periodical, like the *National Geographic*. In order to hook Western sympathies and enlist Western support, such an article, I figured, should include the horrors from which these refugees had escaped. Stories of appalling inhumanity and torture on the part of the Chinese occupation had come to me only peripherally, in snatches, from laypeople and other Westerners. The Rinpoches themselves were reluctant to describe or discuss them.

I presented my argument to Choegyal Rinpoche, the most accessible and confiding of the tulkus. He had been a mature thirteen-year-old when the soldiers invaded his monastery, and he had his own memories to tap of what they had done to his monks and lamas. I suspected a voyeuristic element in my eagerness to hear the ghastly tales—a voyeurism bred by the yellow journalism of Sunday supplements in my New York childhood, and by horror movies of arcane Chinese torture. Still I knew that such accounts would arrest the attention of Western readers and rally support for the Tibetan cause.

Only when I convinced Choegyal that sharing these memories with the Western public would aid the plight of Tibetan refugees did he begin to disclose some of what he had seen and suffered at the hands of the Chinese before his flight from Tibet. The stories came in snatches of conversations, as we paused outside the new craft production center or walked over to the monastery in its temporary, rented quarters. Then only did he divulge some elements of what had occurred. Many of these elements, the forms of intimidation, coercion, and torture employed, have become public knowledge by now, although reports from Amnesty International and the International Council of Jurists may not have the heart-churning immediacy of Choegyal's words. The lesson I learned, however, and that will stay forever with me, is not about the human capacity for cruelty.

I was standing with Choegyal under a rhododendron tree, the sunlight flickering on his face through the leaves and through blossoms the color of his robes. He had just divulged what must have been the most painful of his memories—what the Chinese military had done to his monks in the great prayer hall, as his teachers hid him on the mountainside above the monastery. I gasped with shock, and breathed hard to contain the grief and anger that arose in me. Then I was stilled by the look he turned on me, with eyes that shone with unshed tears.

"Poor Chinese," he murmured.

With a shudder of acknowledgment, I realized that the tears in his eyes were not for himself or for his monks or for his once great monastery of Dugu in the land of Kham in Eastern Tibet. Those tears were for the destroyers themselves.

"Poor Chinese," he said, "they make such bad karma for themselves."

I cannot emulate that reach of compassion, but I have seen it. I have recognized it. I know now that it is within our human capacity. And that changes for me the face of life.

THE SHAMBHALA WARRIORS 11

I OFTEN TELL THIS STORY in workshops, for it describes the work we aim to do and the training we engage in. It is from a prophecy that arose in Tibetan Buddhism over twelve centuries ago. I learned of it from my Tibetan friends in India when, on a visit in 1980, I heard some of them speak of this ancient prophecy as coming true in our time. The signs it foretold, they said, are recognizable now, in our generation. Since this prophecy speaks of a time of great danger for all beings, I was, as you can imagine, very interested to find out about it.

There are varying interpretations of this prophecy. Some portray the coming of the kingdom of Shambhala as an internal event, a metaphor for one's inner spiritual journey independent of the world around us. Others present it as an entirely external event that will unfold in our world independent of what we may choose to do or what our participation may be in the healing of our world. A third version of the prophecy was given to me by my friend and teacher Choegyal Rinpoche of the Tashi Jong community in northern India.

The Prophecy

There comes a time when all life on Earth is in danger. Great barbarian powers have arisen. Although these powers spend their wealth in preparations to annihilate each other, they have much in common: weapons of unfathomable destructive power, and technologies that lay waste to our world. In this time, when the future of all sentient life hangs by the frailest of threads, the kingdom of Shambhala emerges.

Now you can't go there, for it is not a place. It is not a geopolitical entity. It exists in the hearts and minds of the Shambhala warriors. But you cannot recognize a Shambhala warrior by sight, for there is no uniform or insignia, no flags. They have no barricades on which to climb and threaten the enemy, or behind which they can rest and regroup. They have no home turf, and are always moving across the terrain of the barbarians themselves.

Now the time comes when great courage is required of the Shambhala warriors—moral and physical courage. For they must go into the very heart of the barbarian power, into the pits and citadels where the weapons are kept in order to dismantle them. To dismantle weapons, in every sense of the word, they must go into the corridors of power where decisions are made.

The Shambhala warriors know they can do this because the weapons are *manomaya*. They are "mind-made." Made by the human mind, they can be unmade by the human mind. The Shambhala warriors know that the dangers threatening life on Earth are not visited upon us by extraterrestrial powers or satanic deities. They arise from our own choices, our priorities and relationships.

So in this time, the Shambhala warriors go into training. When Choegyal said this, I asked, "How do they train?" They train, he said, in the use of two weapons. "What weapons?" I asked, and he held up his hands in the way the lamas hold the ritual objects of dorje and bell in the great monastic dances of his people.

The weapons are compassion and insight. Both are necessary, he said. You have to have compassion because it provides the fuel to move you out there to do what is needed. It means not being afraid of the suffering of our world. But that weapon is very hot, and by itself is not enough. It can burn you out, so you need the other—you need insight into the dependent co-arising of all things. With that wisdom you know that it is not a battle between the good guys and the bad guys, for the line between good and evil runs through the landscape of every human heart. And with that insight, you also know that each action undertaken with pure intent has repercussions throughout the web of life, beyond what you can measure or discern. By itself, that insight can seem too cool, too conceptual to sustain you and keep you moving, so you need the heat of the compassion, our openness to the world's pain. Both are necessary to the Shambhala warrior.

Taking Heart:
Spiritual Practices for Activists 12

You and I are flowers of a tenacious family.
Breathe slowly and deeply,
Free of previous occupation.
The latest good news
Is that you can do it,
And that I can take time to do it too, with you.
—MARCI THURSTON SHAINE

T O HEAL OUR SOCIETY, our psyches must heal as well. Haunted by the desperate needs of our time and beset by more commitments than we can easily carry, we may wonder how to find the time and energy for spiritual disciplines. Few of us feel free to take to the cloister or the meditation cushion to seek personal transformation.

We do not need to withdraw from the world or spend long hours in solitary prayer or meditation to begin to wake up to the spiritual power within us. The activities and encounters of our daily lives can serve as the occasion for that kind of discovery. I would like to share five simple exercises that can help in this.

The exercises—on death, loving kindness, compassion, mutual power, and mutual recognition—happen to be adapted from the Buddhist tradition. As part of our planetary heritage, they belong to us all. No belief system is necessary, only a readiness to attend to the immediacy of our own experience. They will be most useful if read slowly with a quiet mind (a few deep breaths will help), and if put directly into practice as you go about your day. If you read them aloud for others or put them on tape, allow several seconds of breath and pause throughout.

Meditation on Death

Most spiritual paths ask us to confront the transiency of human life. Medieval Christians honored this in the mystery play of *Everyman*. Don Juan, the Yaqui sorcerer, taught that the enlightened warrior walks with death at his shoulder. To confront and accept the inevitability of our dying releases us from attachments and frees us to live boldly.

An initial meditation on the Buddhist path involves reflection on the twofold fact that: "death is certain" and "the time of death is uncertain." The massive dangers overshadowing our world today, including nuclear warheads still targeted and "on alert," serve that meditation, for they tell us we can die together at any moment, without warning. When we allow that possibility to become conscious, it is painful, but it also jolts us awake to life's vividness, its miraculous quality, heightening our awareness of the beauty and uniqueness of each object and each being. As an occasional practice in daily life:

Look at the person you encounter (stranger or friend). This person lives on an endangered planet. He or she may die in a nuclear war, or from the poisons spreading through our world. Observe that face, unique, vulnerable . . . Those eyes still can see. . . . the skin is still intact . . . Become aware of your desire that this person be spared such suffering and horror, feel the strength of that desire, . . . keep breathing . . . Also let the possibility arise in your consciousness that this may be the person you happen to be with when you die . . . that face the last you see . . . that hand the last you touch . . . it might reach out to help you then, to comfort, to give water . . . Open to the feelings for this person that surface in you with the awareness of this possibility . . . Open to the levels of caring and connection it reveals in you.

Meditation on Loving Kindness

On the Buddhist path, loving kindness, or *metta,* is the first of the four "Immeasurables," also known as the *Brahmaviharas.* Meditation to arouse and sustain loving kindness is a staple of the Sarvodaya Shramadana Movement for community development in Sri Lanka, and is accorded minutes of silence at the outset of every meeting. Organizers and village workers find it useful in developing motivation for service and overcoming feelings of hostility or inadequacy in themselves and others.

I first received instruction in this meditation from a nun in the Tibetan Buddhist tradition. Here is a version that I have adapted for use in the West.

Close your eyes and begin to relax, exhaling to expel tension. Now center in on the normal flow of the breath, letting go of all extraneous thoughts as you passively watch the breathing-in and breathing-out . . .

Now call to mind someone you love very dearly . . . in your mind's eye see the face of that beloved one . . . silently speak her or his name . . . Feel your love for this being, like a current of energy coming through you . . . Now let yourself experience how much you want this person to be free from fear, how intensely you desire that this person be released from greed and ill-will, from confusion and sorrow and the causes of suffering . . . That desire, in all its sincerity and strength, is metta, the great loving kindness . . .

Continuing to feel that warm current of energy coming through the heart, see in your mind's eye those with whom you share your daily life, family members, close friends and colleagues, the people you live and work with . . . Let them appear now as in a circle around you. Behold them one by one, silently speaking their names . . . and direct to each in turn that same current of loving kindness . . . Among these beings may be some with whom you are uncomfortable, in conflict, or tension. With those especially, experience your desire that each be free from fear, from hatred, free from greed and ignorance and the causes of suffering . . .

Now allow to appear, in wider concentric circles, your relations and your acquaintances . . . Let the beam of loving kindness play on them as well, pausing on the faces that appear randomly in your mind's eye. With them as well, experience how much you want their freedom from greed, fear, hatred, and confusion, how much you want all beings to be happy . . .

Beyond them, in concentric circles that are wider yet, appear now all beings with whom you share this planet-time. Though you have not met, your lives are interconnected in ways beyond knowing. To these beings as well, direct the same powerful current of loving kindness. Experience your desire and your intention that each awaken from fear and hatred, from greed and confusion . . . that all beings be released from suffering . . .

As in the ancient Buddhist meditation, we direct the loving kindness now to all the "hungry ghosts," the restless spirits that are prey still to fear and confusion. May they find rest . . . may they rest in the great loving kindness and in the deep peace it brings . . .

By the power of our imagination let us move out now beyond our planet, out into the universe, into other solar systems, other galaxies, other Buddha fields. The current of loving kindness is not affected by physical distances, and we direct it now, as if aiming a beam of light, to all centers of conscious life . . . To all sentient beings everywhere we direct our heartfelt wish that they, too, be free of fear and greed, of hatred and confusion and the causes of suffering . . . May all beings be happy . . .

Now, from out there in the interstellar distances, we turn and behold our own planet, our home . . . We see it suspended there in the blackness of space, blue and white jewel planet turning in the light of its sun . . . Slowly we approach it, drawing nearer, nearer, returning to this region of it, this very place . . . And as you approach this place, let yourself see the being you know best of all . . . the person it has been given you to be in this lifetime . . . You know this person better than anyone else does, know its pain and its hopes, know its need for love, know how hard it tries . . . Let the face of this being, your own face, appear before you . . . Speak the name you are called in love . . . And experience, with that same strong energy-current of loving kindness, how deeply you desire that this being be free from fear, released from greed and hatred, liberated from ignorance and confusion and the causes of suffering . . . The great loving kindness linking you to all beings is now complete, because it is directed to your own self as well .

Breathing Through

Basic to most spiritual traditions, as well as to the systems view of the world, is the recognition that we are not separate, isolated entities, but integral and organic parts of the vast web of life. As such, we are like neurons in a neural net through which flow currents of awareness of what is happening to us, as a species and as a planet. In that context, the pain we feel for our world is a living testimony to our interconnectedness with it. If we deny this pain, we become like blocked and atrophied neurons, deprived of life's flow and weakening the larger body in which we take being. But if we let it move through us, we affirm our belonging; our collective awareness increases. We can open to the pain of the world in confidence that it can neither shatter nor isolate us, for we are not objects that can break. We are resilient patterns within a vaster web of knowing.

Because we have been conditioned to view ourselves as separate, competitive, and thus fragile entities, it takes practice to relearn this kind of resilience. A good way to begin is by practicing simple openness, as in the exercise of "breathing through," adapted from an ancient Buddhist meditation for the development of compassion.

Closing your eyes, focus attention on your breathing. Don't try to breathe any special way, slow or long, just watch the breathing as it happens . . . in and out . . . Note the sensations at the nostrils or upper lip, in the chest or abdomen. Stay passive and alert . . .

As you watch the breath, note that it happens by itself, without your will, without your deciding each time to inhale or exhale . . . It's as though you're being breathed—being breathed by life . . . Just as everyone in this room, in this city, in this planet now, is being breathed, sustained in a vast, breathing web of life . . .

Now visualize your breath as a stream or ribbon of air passing through you. See it flow up through your nose, down through your windpipe and into your lungs. Now from your lungs take it through your heart. Picture it flowing through your heart and out through an opening there to reconnect with the larger web of life. Let the breath-stream, as it passes through you, appear as one loop within that vast web, connecting you with it . . .

Now open your awareness to the suffering that is present in the world. Drop for now all defenses and open to your knowledge of that suffering. Let it come as concretely as you can, in images of your fellow beings in prisons, hospitals, slums, refugee camps, scenes of war . . . no need to strain for these images, they are present in you by virtue of our mutual belonging. Relax and just let them surface . . . the vast and countless hardships of our fellow humans, and of our animal brothers and sisters as well, as they swim the seas and fly the air of this ailing planet . . . Now breathe in the pain like dark granules on the stream of air, up through your nose, down through your trachea, lungs, and heart, and out again into the world net . . . You are asked to do nothing for now, but let it pass through your heart . . . Be sure that stream flows through and out again; don't hang on to the pain . . . surrender it for now to the healing resources of life's vast web . . .

With Shantideva, the Buddhist saint, we can say, "Let all sorrows ripen in me." We help them ripen by passing them through our hearts . . . making good rich compost out of all that grief . . . so we can learn from it, enhancing our larger, collective knowing . . .

If no images or feelings arise and there is only blankness, grey and numb, breathe that through. The numbness itself is a very real part of our world . . .

And if what surfaces for you is not the pain of other beings so much as your own personal suffering, breathe that through, too. Your own anguish is an inextricable part of the grief of our world, and arises with it . . .

Should you feel an ache in the chest, a pressure in the rib cage, as if the heart would break, that is all right. Your heart is not an object that can break . . . But if it were, they say the heart that breaks open can hold the whole universe. Your heart is that large. Trust it. Keep breathing . . .

This guided meditation serves to introduce the process of breathing through, which, once familiar, becomes useful in daily life in the many situations that confront us with suffering. By breathing through the bad news, rather than bracing ourselves against it, we can let it strengthen our sense of belonging in the larger web of being. It helps us remain alert and open, whether reading the newspaper, receiving criticism, or simply being present to a person in pain.

For activists working for peace and justice, and those dealing firsthand with the griefs of our time, the practice helps prevent burnout.

Reminding us of the collective nature of both our problems and our power, it offers a healing measure of humility. It can save us from self-righteousness. For when we can take in our world's pain, accepting it as the price of our caring, we let it inform our acts without needing to inflict it as a punishment on others who seem less involved.

The Great Ball of Merit

Compassion, which is grief in the grief of others, is but one side of the coin. The other side is joy in the joy of others—which in Buddhism is called *mudita*. To the extent that we allow ourselves to identify with the sufferings of other beings, we are able to identify with their strengths as well. This is very important for a sense of adequacy and resilience, because we face a time of great challenge that demands of us more commitment, endurance and courage than we can dredge up out of our individual supply. We can learn to draw on the other neurons in the neural net, and view them in a grateful and celebratory fashion, as so much "money in the bank."

This practice is adapted from the *Meditation of Jubilation and Transformation,* taught in a Buddhist text written two thousand years ago at the outset of the Mahayana tradition. You can find the original version in chapter six of the *Perfection of Wisdom in 8,000 Lines.* I find it very useful today in two forms. The one closer to the ancient practice is this:

> Relax and close your eyes. Open your awareness to the fellow beings who share with you this planet-time . . . in this town . . . in this country . . . and in other lands . . . See their multitudes in your mind's eye . . . Now let your awareness open wider yet, to encompass all beings who ever lived . . . of all races and creeds and walks of life, rich, poor, kings and beggars, saints and sinners . . . see the vast vistas of these fellow beings stretching into the distance, like successive mountain ranges . . . You know that in each of these innumerable lives some act of merit was performed.

No matter how stunted or deprived the life, there was a gesture of generosity, a gift of love, an act of valor or self-sacrifice . . . on the battlefield or workplace, hospital or home . . . From these beings in their endless multitudes arose actions of courage and kindness, of teaching and healing. Let yourself see these manifold and immeasurable acts of merit . . .

Now imagine you can sweep together these acts of merit . . . sweep them into a pile in front of you . . . use your hands . . . pile them up . . . pile them into a heap, beholding it with gladness and gratitude . . . Now pat them into a ball. It is the Great Ball of Merit . . . hold it now and weigh it in your hands . . . rejoice in it, knowing that no act of goodness is ever lost. It remains ever and always a present resource . . . a means for the transformation of life . . . So now, with jubilation and gratitude, you turn that great ball . . . turn it over . . . over . . . into the healing of our world.

As we can learn from contemporary science and visualize in the holographic model of reality, our lives interpenetrate. In the fluid tapestry of space-time, there is at root no distinction between self and other. The acts and intentions of others are like seeds that can germinate and bear fruit through our own lives, as we take them into awareness and dedicate, or "turn over," that awareness to our own empowerment. Thoreau, Gandhi, Martin Luther King, Dorothy Day, and countless nameless heroes and heroines of our own day, all can be part of our Ball of Merit, from which we can draw inspiration and endurance. Other traditions feature notions similar to this, such as the "cloud of witnesses" of which St. Paul spoke, or the Treasury of Merit in the Catholic Church.

The second, more workaday version of the Ball of Merit meditation helps us open to the powers in people around us. It is in direct contrast to the commonly accepted, patriarchal notion of power as something personally owned and exerted over others. The exercise prepares us to bring expectant attention to our encounters with other beings, to view them with fresh openness and curiosity as to how they can enhance our Ball of Merit. We can play this inner game with someone opposite us on the bus or across the bargaining table. It is especially useful when dealing with a person with whom we may be in conflict.

What does this person add to my Great Ball of Merit? What gifts of intellect can enrich our common store? What reserves of stubborn endurance can she or he offer? What flights of fancy or powers of love lurk behind those eyes? What kindness or courage hides in that face, what healing in those hands?

Opening ourselves to the presence of these strengths, we inhale our awareness of them, as in the breathing-through exercise. As our awareness grows, we experience our gratitude for them and our capacity to partake.

Often we let our perceptions of the powers of others make us feel inadequate. Alongside an eloquent colleague, we can feel inarticulate; in the presence of an athlete we can feel weak and clumsy; and we can come to resent both ourself and the other person. In the light of the Great Ball of Merit, however, the gifts and good fortune of others appear not as competing challenges, but as resources we can honor and take pleasure in. We can learn to play detective, spying out treasures for the enhancement of life from even the unlikeliest material. Like air, and sun, and water, they form part of our common good.

In addition to releasing us from the mental cramp of envy, this spiritual practice offers two other rewards. One is pleasure in our own acuity as our merit-detecting ability improves. The second is the response of others who, though ignorant of the game we are playing, sense something in our manner that invites them to disclose more of the person they can be.

Learning to See Each Other

This exercise is derived from the Buddhist practice of the Brahmaviharas, also known as the Four Immeasurables, which are loving kindness, compassion, joy in the joy of others, and equanimity. Adapted for use in a social context, it helps us to see each other more truly and experience the depths of our interconnectedness.

In groups, I offer this as a guided meditation with participants sitting in pairs facing each other. Each serves as a "meditation object" for the other. At the close, I encourage them to proceed to use it, or any portion they like, as they go about their daily lives. It is an excellent antidote to boredom, when our eye falls on another person, say on the subway, or waiting in the checkout line. It charges that idle moment with beauty and discovery. It also is useful when dealing with people whom we are tempted to dislike or disregard; it breaks open our accustomed ways of viewing them. When used like this, as a meditation-in-action, one does not, of course, gaze long and deeply at the other, as in the guided exercise. A seemingly casual glance is enough. The guided, group form goes like this:

Sit in pairs, facing each other without speaking. Take in each other's presence as fully as you can. You may never see this person again: the opportunity to behold the uniqueness of this particular human being is given to you now . . .

As you behold this person, think of the powers that are there . . . Open your awareness to the gifts and strengths and the potentialities in this being . . . Behind those eyes are unmeasured reserves of courage and intelligence . . . of creativity, endurance, wit, and wisdom . . . There are gifts there, of which this person her/himself is not yet aware . . . Consider what these powers could do for the healing of our planet, if they were believed and acted on . . . As you consider that, feel your desire that this person be free from fear . . . Experience how much you want this being to be free from fear, free from greed, released from hatred and from sorrow and from the causes of suffering . . . Know that what you are now experiencing is the great loving kindness . . .

Now, sustaining your attention, open to the pain that is in

this person's life. As in all human lives, there is suffering in this one. Though you can only guess at their forms, there are disappointments, failures, losses, loneliness, abuse . . . there are hurts beyond the telling. . . . Let yourself open to that pain, to hurts that this person may never have told another being . . . You cannot take those hurts away; you are not that powerful. But what you can do is be unafraid to be with them. As you let yourself simply be present with that suffering, know that what you are experiencing is the great compassion. It is very good for the healing of our world . . .

Now, with this person before you, consider how good it would be to work together . . . on a joint project, toward a common goal . . . to be taking risks together . . . conspiring together and laughing together . . . celebrating the little successes along the way, consoling each other over the setbacks, forgiving each other when you make mistakes . . . and simply being there for each other. . . . As you open to that possibility, what you open to is the great wealth: the pleasure in each other's powers, the joy in each other's joy. . . .

Lastly, let your awareness drop deeper within you, like a stone, sinking below the level of what words can express, to the web of relations that underlies all experience. It is the web of life in which you have taken being, in which you are supported, and that interweaves us through all space and time . . . See the being before you as if seeing the face of one who, at another time, another place, was your lover or your enemy, your parent or your child . . . And now you meet again on this brink of time . . . And you know your lives are as intricately interwoven as nerve cells in the mind of a great being . . . Out of that vast net you cannot fall . . . no stupidity or failure or cowardice can ever sever you from that living web. For that is what you are . . . rest in that knowing. Rest in the Great Peace. . . . Out of it we can act, we can dare anything . . . and let every encounter be a homecoming to our true nature. . . . Indeed it is so . . .

In doing this exercise we realize that we do not have to be particularly noble or saint-like in order to wake up to the power of our connection with other beings. In our time, that simple awakening is the gift the global crises hold for us. For all its horror and stupidity, nuclear war, like the toxins we spew into our world, is also the manifestation of an awesome spiritual truth—the truth about the hell we create for ourselves when we cease to learn how to love. Saints, mystics, and prophets throughout the ages saw that law; now *all* can see it and none can escape its consequences. So we are caught now in a narrow place where we realize that Lao-tzu, the Buddha, Jesus, Mohammed, and our own hearts were right all along; and we are as scared and frantic as a cornered rat, and as dangerous. But if we let it, that narrow cul-de-sac can turn into a birth canal, pressing and pushing us through the darkness of pain, until we are delivered into . . . what? Love seems too weak a word. It is, as Saint Paul said, "the glory to be revealed in us." It stirs in us now.

For us to regard the threat of nuclear war, the dying seas, or the poisoned air as a monstrous injustice suggests that we never took seriously the injunction to love. Perhaps we thought all along that Gautama and Jesus were kidding, or their teachings were meant only for saints. But now comes the daunting revelation, that we are *all* called to be saints—not good necessarily, or pious, or devout—but saints in the sense of just caring for each other. One wonders what terrors this knowledge must hold that we fight it so, and flee from it in such pain. Can our present capacity to extinguish all life tell us this? Can it force us to face the terrors of love? Can it be the occasion of our birth?

In that possibility we take heart. Even in confusion and fear, with all our fatigues and petty faults, we can let that awareness work in and through our lives. Such simple exercises as those offered here can help us do that, can help us begin to see our self and each other with fresh eyes.

PART THREE:

Sowing Seeds for the Future

THE GREAT TURNING   13

If we will have the wisdom to survive
to stand like slow growing trees
on a ruined place, renewing, enriching it
then a long time after we are dead
the lives our lives prepare
will live here.
—WENDELL BERRY

THE TURNING WHEEL IS a powerful symbol of the mystery at the heart of life. Planets, solar systems, and electrons in their orbits are wheels revolving within larger wheels, just as the hours and seasons of day and year rotate. As circulation of the blood flows rhythmically through the body, so do vast hydrological and carbon cycles sustain our living world. Like the sacred hoop of the Native Americans and the round dances and mandalas of ancient peoples, the wheel reminds us that all is alive and moving, interconnected and intersecting. Little wonder, then, that the wheel has served to symbolize the Dharma. For the Buddha taught, in his central doctrine, the dependent co-arising of all things, how they continually change and condition each other in interconnections as real as the spokes in a wheel. Thus, when he taught, he was said to turn the Wheel of the Dharma.

In this book, two Turnings of the Wheel of the Dharma are described. The first occurred when the Buddha first taught the radical interdependence of all things. The second Turning occurred at the beginning of the Mahayana, when scriptures honoring the Perfection of Wisdom, or Mother of All Buddhas, returned to that central doctrine and cast it in new perspectives and fresh forms. Now, I suggest, the cognitive shifts and spiritual openings taking place in our own time can be seen as the third Turning of the Wheel, a dramatic re-emergence of the Dharma of dependent co-arising.

The recognition of our essential non-separateness from the world, beyond the shaky walls erected by our fear and greed, is a gift occurring in countless lives in every generation. Yet there are historical moments when this recognition breaks through on a more collective level. This is happening now in ways that converge to bring into question the very foundation and direction of our civilization. A global revolution is occurring that is of such magnitude that people unacquainted with Buddhism are using a similar term. Many are calling it the Great Turning.

Toward a Life-honoring Civilization

Corporate-controlled media are not reporting this tidal change, but once we learn to see it, our time in history no longer appears as some grim hopeless fate in which we are trapped. It becomes a great adventure that can invigorate and ennoble every aspect of life. It is the epochal shift from the industrial growth society to a life-sustaining society. And it is a matter of survival.

This revolution begins with the acknowledgment of two facts. First, that an economic system that depends on ever-increasing corporate profits—on how fast the Earth can be turned into consumer goods, weapons, and waste—is suicidal. And second, that our needs can be met without destroying our world. We have technology and resources available to produce sufficient food and energy, ensure clean air and water, and leave a livable world for those who come after us.

Future generations, if we leave them the means to exist, will look back on these early years of the twenty-first century as the time of

Great Turning. I imagine they will say, "Those ancestors back then, bless them. Though working to save life on Earth, they had no way of knowing if they could pull it off. It must have looked hopeless at times. Their efforts must have often seemed isolated, diffuse, darkened by confusion. Yet they went ahead, they kept on doing what they could, and because they kept on, the Great Turning happened."

Wherever I go these days, in every group I meet with, the Great Turning becomes more useful as a conceptual frame. It identifies the shift from a self-destroying political economy to one in harmony with Earth and enduring for the future. It unites and includes all the actions being taken to honor and preserve life on Earth.

Of course, not everyone involved in this adventure calls it the Great Turning. You don't need that name in order to fight for survival and fashion the forms of a sane and decent future. Yet, more and more of us are finding the concept to be both accurate and inspiring. For me, as a teacher, activist, and grandmother, the Great Turning helps me see what the physical eye cannot. It illumines the larger forces at play and the direction they are taking. At the same time, it sharpens my perception of the actual, concrete ways people are engaging in this global transformation. In other words, it serves as both compass and lens.

The Big Picture

From the countless social and environmental issues that compete for attention, we can take on isolated causes and fight for them with courage and devotion. But the forces we confront seem so great and time so short, it's easy to fear that our efforts are too scattered to be of real consequence. We tend to fall into the same short-term thinking that has entrapped our political economy.

The Great Turning invites us to lift our eyes from the cramped closet of short-term thinking and see the broader historical landscape. What a difference it makes to view our efforts as part of a vaster enterprise. What is underway, as many have observed, is a revolution that is comparable in magnitude to the agricultural revolution of the late Neolithic era ten thousand years ago and the industrial revolution of the past two-and-a-half centuries. The first one took centuries to unfold. The second only took generations. Right on its heels, as the industrial growth society spins out of control, comes this third revolution which thinkers have referred to as the environmental or ecological or sustainability revolution. As they point out, this transition must happen not in centuries or generations, but within a matter of years. That is because we have exceeded the limits of what the Earth can restore and absorb. In systems terms, our economy is on "overshoot" and exponential "runaway." While having to occur in a shorter time, it must also be more thorough-going—involving not only our institutions and technologies, but also the attitudes and habits that sustain them.

William Ruckelshaus, first director of the Environmental Protection Agency, reflected that while the first two revolutions "were gradual, spontaneous, and largely unconscious, this [third] one will have to be a fully conscious operation. If we actually do it, the undertaking will be absolutely unique in humanity's stay on Earth."

As compass, the Great Turning helps us see the direction in which our political economy is headed. Because it is based on an impossible imperative—limitless increase in corporate profits—its trajectory leads to collapse. No system can endure which seeks to maximize a single variable. No possibility exists for unlimited growth in a finite planet. To quote Gus Speth, former head of the United Nations Development Program, "Our world, our only habitat, is a biotic system under such stress that it threatens to fail in fundamental and irreversible ways."

Yet life is a dynamic process, self-organizing to adapt and evolve. Just as it turned scales to feathers, gills to lungs, seawater to blood, so now, too, immense evolutionary forces are at work. They are driving this revolution of ours through innumerable, molecular, intersecting alterations in the human capacity for conscious change.

No Guarantee

As Earth's record attests, extinctions are as plentiful as successful adaptations. We may not make it this time. Natural systems may unravel beyond repair before new sustainable forms and structures take hold. This is part of the anguish that is widely felt.

That anguish is unavoidable if we want to stay honest and alert. The Great Turning comes with no guarantees. Its risk of failure is its reality. Insisting on belief in a positive outcome puts blinders on us and burdens the heart. We might manage to convince ourselves that everything will surely turn out all right; but would such a positive prediction elicit our greatest courage and creativity?

When you make peace with uncertainty, you find a kind of liberation. You are freed from bracing yourself against every piece of bad news, and from constantly having to work up a sense of hopefulness in order to act—which can be exhausting. There's a certain equanimity and moral economy that comes when you are not constantly computing your chance of success. The enterprise is so vast, there is no way to judge the effects of this or that individual effort—or the extent to which it makes any difference at all. Once we acknowledge this, we can enjoy the challenge and the adventure. Then we can see that it is a privilege to be alive now in this Great Turning, when all the wisdom and courage ever harvested can be put to use.

Three Dimensions

Let us look at how the Great Turning is happening. It unfolds in three simultaneous and mutually reinforcing dimensions. Recognize how they are revolving through your own life, gaining momentum through the choices you make and the visions you nourish.

I. HOLDING ACTIONS

Here we find what is generally called "activism." It is all the political, legislative, legal, and regulatory work undertaken to slow down the destruction inflicted by the industrial growth society, and also includes blockades, boycotts, civil disobedience, and other forms of refusal. Often confronting active opposition from government and industry, this dimension encompasses a wide variety of actions, such as:

- ▶ resistance to oil drilling, forest clear cutting, police brutality, toxic waste;
- ▶ citizen monitoring, litigation, and testimony in public hearings for enforcement of social and environmental regulations;
- ▶ the creation of soup kitchens, shelters, free clinics for the homeless;
- ▶ support for the human and civil rights of immigrants;
- ▶ whistle-blowing on illegal and unethical corporate and governmental practices;
- ▶ protesting U.S. military occupations and state-sponsored torture.

Work in this dimension buys time. It saves lives. It saves some species, ecosystems, and cultures. It preserves some of the gene pool for the future. It provides a laboratory for new kinds of decentralized organizing and consensus-based decision-making. Although insufficient by itself to bring about an alternative society, it is necessary to the preservation of life.

Let's face it: this first dimension is wearing. You can get stressed out of your mind by nonstop crises, the constant searching for funding, the battles lost, and the increasing violence against activists. When you step back to take a breather, you often feel as if you are abandoning ship. But this is not the case. You can continue the work of the Great Turning in other forms—the way the head goose, when she's tired, slips back and flies in the wind stream of others, and another flyer takes her place.

II. Structural Change

To free ourselves and our planet from the industrial growth society, we must understand its dynamics. What are the political and economic structures that lead us to use our Earth as supply house and sewer?

What are the tacit agreements creating obscene wealth for a few, while the majority of humanity sinks into poverty and want? A few years ago, it was hard slogging to raise public interest in the North American Free Trade Agreement (NAFTA) or the International Monetary Fund (IMF); people's eyes glazed over. But now, as an upsurge of books, articles, teach-ins, and demonstrations demystifies the workings of the global economy, we are wising up. Informed public attention and resistance movements are both local and global.

Clarity as to how the old system works helps us see how it can be replaced. Alternative institutions and ways of doing things are mushrooming, from local currencies to consumer cooperatives, from eco-villages to community-supported agriculture (CSA). At no other epoch of human history have so many new ways of doing things appeared in so short a time. They may *look* marginal to us today, but they hold the seeds of the future. A few more examples:

- ▶ new indices of wealth and prosperity, sustainability indicators to replace the Gross Domestic Product, which ignores ecological and human health;
- ▶ renewable energy technologies from wind to solar, biomass, and tidal;
- ▶ new forms of land ownership such as land trusts and conservancies;
- ▶ holistic health practices that enlist the self-organizing powers of body and mind;
- ▶ permaculture, farmers' markets, urban gardens, and other healthy sustainable ways of growing food.

Yet, as promising as they are, these forms and structures cannot survive without deeply rooted values to nourish them. To proliferate and endure, they must mirror a profound change in our perception of reality.

III. SHIFT IN CONSCIOUSNESS

A paradigmatic shift—the third dimension of the Great Turning—is happening all around us. We are becoming aware of the web of relationships in which we have our being. We are helped by new discoveries in science, revealing that Earth is not inert matter to be used as a commodity, but a living system in which we are intricately interconnected. This cognitive revolution is paralleled by a spiritual one. Ancient teachings become available to us now, showing us the beauty and power that can be ours as conscious, responsible members of the living body of Earth. Like our ancestors, we begin again to see the world as our body, and, whether we say the word or not, as sacred. The forms of this awakening are many. Among them are:

- ▸ living systems theory, revealing the self-organizing nature of reality and the presence of mind in nature;
- ▸ Gaia theory, showing our planet to be a living system and our larger body;
- ▸ the deep, long-range ecology movement retrieving us from anthropocentrism and restoring our community with all life forms;
- ▸ Liberation Theology and Creation Spirituality, which breach dichotomies erected by hierarchical religious thought, and invoke the sanctity of all life;
- ▸ ecofeminism, blending political critique with women's spirituality movement, refiguring reality in radical relational terms;
- ▸ ecopsychology, lifting the aims and means of psychotherapy into larger concerns of social pathology;
- ▸ the voluntary simplicity movement, liberating us from life-destroying patterns of consumption.

Though we hardly have words for it, this cognitive, spiritual, and perceptual revolution is occurring at a stunning rate of speed. The late California poet, Robinson Jeffers, captures the flavor of this awakening in the poem:

> I entered the life of the brown forest,
> And the great life of the ancient peaks, the patience of stone,
> I felt the changes in the veins

In the throat of the mountain, and I was the stream
Draining the mountain wood; and I the stag drinking; and I was
    the stars
Boiling with light, wandering alone, each one the lord of his
    own summit;
and I was the darkness
Outside the stars, I included them, they were a part of me.
    I was mankind also, a moving lichen
On the cheek of the round stone . . .
How can I express the excellence I have found,
that has no color but clearness;
No honey but ecstasy . . .

This shift in our sense of identity will be life-saving in the sociopolitical and ecological ordeals that lie before us.

Together, these three dimensions free us from the grip of the industrial growth society. They offer us nobler goals and truer pleasures. They help preserve us from paralysis or panic, when things get hard, so that we can resist the temptation to stick our heads in the sand or seek scapegoats for our fears. They help us move forward with trust in ourselves and each other, so that we can join hands in learning how the world self-heals and regenerates.

The Great Turning turns my face toward the possible and helps me live with radical uncertainty. It causes me to believe that, whether we succeed or not, the risks we take on behalf of life will bring forth dimensions of human intelligence and solidarity beyond any we have known.

The Greening of the Self   14

May we turn inwards and stumble upon our true roots
in the intertwining biology of this exquisite planet.
May nourishment and power pulse through these roots,
and fierce determination to continue the billion-year dance.
—JOHN SEED

SOMETHING IMPORTANT is happening in our world that you will not read about in the newspapers. I consider it the most fascinating and hopeful development of our time, and it is one of the reasons I am so glad to be alive today. It has to do with our notion of the self.

The self is the metaphoric construct of identity and agency, the hypothetical piece of turf on which we construct our strategies for survival, the notion around which we focus our instincts for self-preservation, our needs for self-approval, and the boundaries of our self-interest. Something is shifting here. The conventional notion of the self with which we have been raised and to which we have been conditioned by mainstream culture is being undermined. What Alan Watts called "the skin-encapsulated ego" and Gregory Bateson referred to as "the epistemological error of Occidental civilization" is being peeled off. It is being replaced by wider constructs of identity and self-interest—by what philosopher Arne Naess termed the ecological self, coextensive with other beings and the life of our planet. It is what I like to call "the greening of the self."

Bodhisattvas in Rubber Boats

In a lecture on a college campus some years back, I gave examples of activities being undertaken in defense of life on Earth—actions in which people risk their comfort and even their lives to protect other species. In the Chipko or tree-hugging movement in north India, for example, villagers protect their remaining woodlands from ax and bulldozer by interposing their bodies. On the open seas, Greenpeace activists intervene to protect marine mammals from slaughter. After that talk, I received a letter from a student I'll call Michael. He wrote:

> I think of the tree-huggers hugging my trunk, blocking the chain saws with their bodies. I feel their fingers digging into my bark to stop the steel and let me breathe. I hear the bodhisattvas in their rubber boats as they put themselves between the harpoons and me, so I can escape to the depths of the sea. I give thanks for your life and mine, and for life itself. I give thanks for realizing that I too have the powers of the tree-huggers and the bodhisattvas.

What is striking about Michael's words is the shift in identification. Michael is able to extend his sense of self to encompass the self of the tree and of the whale. Tree and whale are no longer removed, separate, disposable objects pertaining to a world "out there"; they are intrinsic to his own vitality. Through the power of his caring, his experience of self is expanded far beyond that skin-encapsulated ego. I quote Michael's words not because they are unusual, but to the contrary, because they express a desire and a capacity that is being released from the prison-cell of old constructs of self. This desire and capacity are arising in more and more people today, out of deep concern for what is happening to our world, as they begin to speak and act on its behalf.

Among those who are shedding these old constructs of self, like old skin or a confining shell, is John Seed, director of the Rainforest Information Centre in Australia. One day we were walking through the rain forest in New South Wales, where he has his office, and I asked him, "You talk about the struggle against the lumber companies and politicians to save the remaining rain forests. How do you deal with the despair?"

He replied, "I try to remember that it's not me, John Seed, trying to protect the rain forest. Rather, I am part of the rain forest protecting itself. I am that part of the rain forest recently emerged into human thinking." This is what I mean by the greening of the self. It involves a combining of the mystical with the pragmatic, transcending separateness, alienation, and fragmentation. It is a shift that Seed himself calls "a spiritual change," generating a sense of profound interconnectedness with all life.

This is hardly new to our species. In the past, poets and mystics have been speaking and writing about these ideas, but not people on the barricades agitating for social change. Now the sense of an encompassing self, that deep identity with the wider reaches of life, is a motivation for action. It is a source of courage that helps us stand up to the powers that are still, through force of inertia, working for the destruction of our world. This expanded sense of self leads to sustained and resilient action on behalf of life.

When you look at what is happening to our world—and it is hard to look at what's happening to our water, our air, our trees, our fellow species—it becomes clear that unless you have some roots in a spiritual practice that holds life sacred and encourages joyful communion with all your fellow beings, facing the enormous challenges ahead becomes nearly impossible.

Robert Bellah's book *Habits of the Heart* is not a place where you are going to read about the greening of the self. But it is where you will read *why* there has to be a greening of the self, because it describes the cramp that our society has gotten itself into. Bellah points out that the individualism embodied in and inflamed by the industrial growth society is accelerating. It not only causes alienation and fragmentation in our century but also is endangering our survival. Bellah calls for a moral ecology. "We have to treat others as part of who we are," he says, "rather than as a 'them' with whom we are in constant competition."

To Robert Bellah, I respond, "It is happening." It is happening because of three converging developments. First, the conventional small self, or ego-self, is being psychologically and spiritually challenged by confrontation with dangers of mass annihilation. The second force working to dismantle the ego-self is a way of seeing that has arisen out of science. From living systems theory and systems cybernetics emerges a process view of the self as inseparable from the web of relationships that sustain it. The third force is the resurgence in our time of nondualistic spiritualities. Here I write from my own experience with Buddhism, but I also see it happening in other faith traditions, such as the Jewish Renewal Movement, Creation Spirituality in Christianity, and Sufism in Islam, as well as in the appreciation being given to the message of indigenous cultures. These developments are impinging on the self in ways that are helping it to break out of its old boundaries and definitions.

Cracked Open by Grief

The move to a wider, ecological sense of self is in large part a function of the dangers that threaten to overwhelm us. Given news reports pointing to the progressive destruction of our biosphere, awareness grows that the world as we know it may come to an end. The loss of certainty that there will be a future is, I believe, the pivotal psychological reality of our time. Why do I claim that this erodes the old sense of self? Because once we stop denying the crises of our time and let ourselves experience the depth of our own responses to the pain of our world—whether it is the burning of the Amazon rain forest, the famines of Africa, or the homeless in our own cities—the grief or anger or fear we experience cannot be reduced to concerns for our own individual skin. When we mourn the destruction of our biosphere, it is categorically distinct from grief at the prospect of our own personal death.

Planetary anguish lifts us onto another systemic level where we open to collective experience. It enables us to recognize our profound interconnectedness with all beings. Don't apologize if you cry for the burning of the Amazon or the Appalachian mountains stripped open for coal. The sorrow, grief, and rage you feel is a measure of your humanity and your evolutionary maturity. As your heart breaks open there will be room for the world to heal. That is what is happening as we see people honestly confronting the sorrows of our time. And it is an adaptive response.

The crisis that threatens our planet, whether seen in its military, ecological, or social aspect, derives from a dysfunctional and pathological notion of the self. It derives from a mistake about our place in the order of things. It is the delusion that the self is so separate and fragile that we must delineate and defend its boundaries; that it is so small and so needy that we must endlessly acquire and endlessly consume; and that as individuals, corporations, nation-states, or a species, we can be immune to what we do to other beings.

The urge to move beyond such a constricted view of self is not new, of course. Many have felt the imperative to extend their self-interest to embrace the whole. What is notable in our situation is that this extension of identity comes not through a desire to be good or altruistic, but simply to be present and own our pain. And that is why this shift in the sense of self is credible to people. As the poet Theodore Roethke said, "I believe my pain."

Cybernetics of the Self

Twentieth-century science undermined the notion of a self that is distinct from the world it observes and acts upon. Einstein showed that the self's perceptions are determined by its position in relation to other phenomena. And Heisenberg, in his uncertainty principle, demonstrated that its perceptions are changed by the very act of observation.

Systems science goes farther in challenging old assumptions about a separate, continuous self, by showing that there is no logical or scientific basis for construing one part of the experienced world as "me" and the rest as "other." That is so because as open, self-organizing systems, our very breathing, acting, and thinking arise in interaction with our shared world through the currents of matter, energy, and information that move through us and sustain us. In the web of relationships that sustain these activities there is no line of demarcation.

As systems theorists say, there is no categorical "I" set over against a categorical "you" or "it." One of the clearest expositions of this is found in the writings of Gregory Bateson, who says that the process that decides and acts cannot be neatly identified with the isolated subjectivity of the individual or located within the confines of the skin. He contends that "the total self-corrective unit that processes information is a system whose boundaries do not at all coincide with the boundaries either of the body or what is popularly called 'self' or 'consciousness.'" He goes on to say, "The self as ordinarily understood is only a small part of a much larger trial-and-error system which does the thinking, acting, and deciding."

Bateson offers two helpful examples. One is a woodcutter in the process of felling a tree. His hands grip the handle of the ax, there is the head of the ax, the trunk of the tree. Whump, he makes a cut, and then whump, another cut. What is the feedback circuit, where is the information that is guiding that cutting down of the tree? It is a whole circle; you can begin at any point. It moves from the eye of the woodcutter, to the hand, to the ax, and back to the cut in the tree. That self-correcting unit is what is chopping down the tree.

In another illustration, a blind person with a cane is walking along the sidewalk. Tap, tap, whoops, there's a fire hydrant, there's a curb. Who is doing the walking? Where is the self of the blind person? What is doing the perceiving and deciding? The self-corrective feedback circuit includes the arm, the hand, the cane, the curb, and the ear. At that moment, that is the self that is walking. Bateson points out that the self is a false reification of an improperly delimited part of a much larger field of interlocking processes. And he goes on to maintain that "this false reification of the self is basic to the planetary ecological crisis in which we find ourselves. We have imagined that we are a unit of survival and we have to see to our own survival, and we imagine that the unit of survival is the separate individual or a separate species, whereas in reality, through the history of evolution it is the individual plus the environment, the species plus the environment, for they are essentially symbiotic."

The self is a metaphor. We can choose to limit it to our skin, our person, our family, our organization, or our species. We can select its boundaries in objective reality. As Bateson explains, our self-reflexive, purposive consciousness illuminates but a small arc in the currents and loops of knowing that interweave us. It is just as plausible to conceive of mind as coexistent with these larger circuits, with the entire "pattern that connects."

Do not think that to broaden the construct of self in this way will eclipse your distinctiveness or that you will lose your identity like a drop in the ocean. From the systems perspective, the emergence of larger self-organizing patterns and wholes both requires diversity and generates it in turn. Integration and differentiation go hand in hand. "As you let life live through you," poet Roger Keyes says, you just become "more of who you really are."

Spiritual Breakthroughs

The third factor that helps dismantle the conventional notion of the self as small and separate is the resurgence of nondualistic spiritualities. This trend can be found in all faith traditions. I have found Buddhism to be distinctive for the clarity and sophistication it brings to understanding the dynamics of the self. In much the same way as systems theory does, Buddhism undermines the dichotomy between self and other and belies the concept of a continuous, self-existent entity. It then goes farther than systems theory in showing the pathogenic character of any reifications of the self. It goes farther still in offering methods for transcending these difficulties and healing this suffering. What the Buddha woke up to under the bodhi tree was paticca samuppada: the dependent co-arising of all phenomena, in which you cannot isolate a separate, continuous self.

Over the eons, in every religion, we have wondered: "What do we do with the self, this clamorous 'I,' always wanting attention, always wanting its goodies? Should we crucify, sacrifice, and mortify it? Or should we affirm, improve, and ennoble it?"

The Buddhist path leads us to realize that all we need to do with the self is see through it. It's just a convention, a convenient convention, to be sure, but with no greater reality than that. When you take it too seriously, when you suppose that it is something enduring which you have to defend and promote, it becomes the foundation of delusion, the motive behind our attachments and aversions.

For a beautiful illustration of how this works in a positive feedback loop, consider the Tibetan wheel of life. Pictured there are the various realms of beings, and at the center of that wheel of samsara are three figures: the snake, the rooster, and the pig—delusion, greed, and aversion—and they just chase each other round and round. The linchpin is the notion of our self, the notion that we have to protect that self or promote it or do *something* with it.

Oh, the sweetness of realizing: I am not other than what I'm experiencing. I am this breathing. I am this moment, and it is changing, continually arising in the fountain of life. We are not doomed to the perpetual rat race of self-protection and self-advancement. The vicious circle can be broken by the wisdom, prajna, of seeing that "self" is just an idea; by the practice of meditation, *dhyana,* which sustains that insight; and by the practice of morality, *sila,* where attention to our actions can free them from bondage to a separate self. Far from the nihilism and escapism often imputed to the Buddhist path, this liberation puts one *into* the world with a livelier sense of social engagement.

Our pain for the world reveals our true nature as one with the entirety of life. The one who knows that is the bodhisattva—and we're all capable of it. Each one can recognize and act upon our inter-existence with all beings. When we turn our eyes away from that homeless figure, are we indifferent or is the pain of seeing him or her too great? Do not be easily duped about the apparent indifference of those around you. What looks like apathy is really fear of suffering. But the bodhisattva knows that if you're afraid to get close to the pain of our world you'll be banished from its joy as well.

One thing I love about the ecological self is that it makes moral exhortation irrelevant. Sermonizing is both boring and ineffective. This is pointed out by Arne Naess, the Norwegian philosopher who coined the terms "deep ecology" and "ecological self."

Naess explains that we change the way we experience our self through an ever-widening process of identification. Borrowing from the Hindu tradition, he calls this process *self-realization:* a progression "where the self to be realized extends further and further beyond the separate ego and includes more and more of the phenomenal world." And he says:

> In this process, notions such as altruism and moral duty are left behind. It is tacitly based on the Latin term "ego" which has as its opposite the "alter." Altruism implies that the ego sacrifices its interests in favor of the other, the *alter*. The motivation is primarily that of duty. It is said we *ought* to love others as strongly as we love our self. There are, however, very limited numbers among humanity capable of loving from mere duty or from moral exhortation.
>
> Unfortunately, the extensive moralizing within the ecological movement has given the public the false impression that they are being asked to make a sacrifice—to show more responsibility, more concern, and a nicer moral standard. But all of that would flow naturally and easily if the self were widened and deepened so that the protection of nature was felt and perceived as protection of our very selves.

Note that virtue is *not* required. The emergence of the ecological self, at this point in our history, is required precisely *because* moral exhortation does not work. Sermons seldom hinder us from following our self-interest as we conceive it.

The obvious choice, then, is to extend our notions of self-interest. For example, it would not occur to me to plead with you, "Don't saw off your leg. That would be an act of violence." It wouldn't occur to me (or to you) because your leg is part of your body. Well, so are the trees in the Amazon rain basin. They are our external lungs. We are beginning to realize that the world is our body.

The ecological self, like any notion of selfhood, is a metaphoric construct, useful for what it allows us to perceive and how it helps us to behave. It is dynamic and situational, a perspective we can choose to adopt according to context and need. Note the words: we can choose. Because it's a metaphor and not a rigid category, choices can be made to identify at different moments, with different dimensions or aspects of our systemically interrelated existence—be they dying rivers or stranded refugees or the planet itself. In doing this, the extended self brings into play wider resources—like a nerve cell in a neural net opening to the charge of the other neurons. With this extension comes a sense of buoyancy and resilience. From the wider web in which we take life, inner resources—courage, endurance, ingenuity—flow through us if we let them. They come like an unexpected blessing.

By expanding our self-interest to include other beings in the body of Earth, the ecological self also widens our window on time. It enlarges our temporal context, freeing us from identifying our goals and rewards solely in terms of our present lifetime. The life pouring through us, pumping our heart and breathing through our lungs, did not begin at our birth or conception. Like every particle in every atom and molecule of our bodies, it goes back through time to the first splitting and spinning of the stars.

Thus the greening of the self helps us to reinhabit time and own our story as life on Earth. We were present in the primal flaring forth, and in the rains that streamed down on this still-molten planet, and in the primordial seas. In our mother's womb we remembered that journey, wearing vestigial gills and tail and fins for hands. Beneath the outer layers of our neocortex and what we learned in school, that story is in us—the story of a deep kinship with all life, bringing strengths that we never imagined. When we claim this story as our innermost sense of who we are, a gladness comes that will help us to survive.

Perseverance for the Long Haul: A Dharma Lesson from Tibet   15

*The day's labor grows simple now
and like a holy face
held in my dark hands.*

—RAINER MARIA RILKE

O N THE FLIGHT from Beijing to San Francisco, my husband, our daughter, and I compared memories of the seven-week trip we had just completed into Tibet. It was late September 1987, just days before the Chinese government's crackdown in Lhasa that would virtually close Tibet to independent foreign travel. We had journeyed on our own through Sichuan province into Kham, the easternmost province of the Autonomous Region of Tibet, to join Tibetan friends whom we'd known for over twenty years in northern India. They were monks and lamas of Tashi Jong, the refugee community in the foothills of the Indian Himalayas where, after fleeing the Chinese occupation of Tibet, they had preserved their culture in exile.

A shift in Chinese policy in the early 1980s had allowed them to return to Tibet—some to visit, some to stay. We had gone to meet them on their home turf and visit the ruins of their monasteries. We had gone to see with our own eyes the land they had so often and vividly described to us. They had asked us to come and see the work they were undertaking to restore their Tibetan Buddhist culture and economy in the place of its birth, after three long decades of devastation and oppression.

The packs we carried onto the plane for our return flight held rolls of film and sheaves of notes about the Eastern Tibet Self-Help Project, for which we hoped to garner support in the West. Our talk held gratitude and laughter as we recalled our adventures. Yet, as the cabin lights dimmed and passengers dozed, my mind reached for something else underneath the exotic trappings of our trip. I was bringing back adventure stories to recount and a worthy project to serve, but what had I learned on a deeper level?

In my mind's eye, I saw Bon-pa Tulku on the earthen ramparts of Khampagar monastery. I whispered the words "Dharma for the Long Haul"—and knew then what I had harvested and would carry back into my life. Here is how this gift was given.

From the main road through Kham, it is a full day's ride to the great monastery of Khampagar. The hills and mountains are much greener there than the arid plateaus of central Tibet. As our caravan of sturdy Khampa ponies left the road behind, we paused on a high grassy shoulder to look back. The road glinted like a ribbon in the morning light, as it curved and cut through the vast green billows of land. "Chinese made," said Nyija, one of the local monks. "Many die." I recalled hearing that forced labor on the road inflicted moral as well as physical suffering, for the Tibetans believed it wrong—bad karma—to blast and cut into the earth. We gazed in silence, then Nyija reached over to adjust my reins and laughed, "We go?" He turned his horse to lead us onward into a terrain less marked by time.

We rode in a company of ten lamas. Above the familiar maroon robes, they wore jaunty, brimmed riding hats which I had only seen in old paintings—white ones for the monks and yellow ones distinguishing the three tulkus or incarnate lamas in our midst. Several among them were old friends from the refugee community of Tashi Jong, like Bon-pa Tulku and Lama Kaju who returned from exile to help rebuild the monastery and teach. Among the rest were monks who had never left Tibet. Some, like Abu Nyendrak Rinpoche, had spent years in prison camps; others, younger, were recently ordained; and one, bright-eyed under a yellow brimmed hat, was a seven-year-old tulku, little Dergen Rinpoche.

Settling into a steady pace, we wound our way single file across the green highlands. Up we rode across slides of shale and hillsides of thick turf, down rocky gullies and up again—most of the journey above the tree line. Wild and majestic expanses spread before our eyes, flickering in the light show made by sun and scudding clouds. Two or three hours from the road brought us into a wide grassy bowl where we spied the black yak-hair tents of nomads. Khampa herders, their long braids wound up in red tassels, strode out to meet us and help us dismount. Fresh-churned yak butter tea had been prepared, and crocks of thick, creamy yak curd, and carpets spread for us to sit on.

Already a little sore from the wooden saddle, it felt good to climb off and stretch and ease my sit-bones on the spongy ground. Our picnic was served with both reverence and humor. Our hosts exchanged news with our party, relaying messages from travelers who had passed through that week. Blocks of cut turf a foot high became seats and tables to honor our Rinpoches. Each of us drank from fine porcelain bowls. I had downed several servings of tea and curds before a sudden low massing of clouds began to spit rain. The drops became a deluge. Amidst laughter our hosts brought out Tibetan raincoats for the three Americans. Huge white circular affairs of heavy matted wool, they were awkward to manage on foot, but once we were hoisted back in the saddle, they covered most of the horse as well as the rider and the effect was stunning. We wore them for the next few miles until the rain eased off.

When the clouds dispersed, high rocky peaks appeared above us, and a dramatic gorge opened to the right, where cliffs as twisting as on a painted scroll plunged down into half-hidden groves of trees. Bon-pa Tulku had us dismount to walk up to the edge and peer over into that dizzying, exquisite scene. Down there, he gestured, hidden in caves and crannies, were ancient treasures of Khampagar monastery.

During the cultural revolution, they had been sequestered by faithful laypeople to save them from destruction by the Red Guards. "Do you know where they are?" I asked. "Not exactly. You see, the people who saved them died. Sometime we will find them."

Remounting, we took a more gentle descent to the left, across an immense grassy hillside strewn with red and purple wildflowers and thick silvery patches of edelweiss. Rivulets sparkled down it to feed into a rushing stream, and where it widened in a flatter stretch, we crossed. Our ponies' hooves slipped on the rocks, splashing and jerking us about, until they clambered up to find dry footing on the opposite bank; then we followed the waterway westward toward a horizon where rose the bare rock peak of a distant mountain. "The mountain over Khampagar," said Bon-pa Tulku, pointing. I glanced at it briefly, then looked back over my shoulder to see how little Dergen Rinpoche had fared in the fording. His horse was riderless. But behind it rode the strapping monk Nyija, and cradled in his arms under a yellow riding hat was a small boy sound asleep.

I stood in my stirrups to tug at the woven saddle carpet, pulling it back again between me and the wooden frame. I thought, "This is the happiest day of my life." To ride along hour after hour in the file of mounted lamas stirred something within me that felt like memory. The steady pace of our Khampa ponies, the jingling of their brass bells amidst the vast surrounding silence, the maroon robes and murmured mantras, all invited me to imagine that I was once again doing what I had done for times as measureless as the land we had entered.

The scenes that our family had struggled through over the past weeks evaporated like a bad dream. The armed Chinese border patrols, the squalid barracks of the People's Liberation Army, the truck compounds awash with mud, oil and excrement, the choking exhaust in the wake of military convoys—they lost reality now, swallowed up into larger and more reassuring dimensions of time.

My mental pictures of Khampagar belonged to those dimensions. I had harvested them at Tashi Jong over the twenty-two years that I had known and worked with the refugee community; for its lamas and laypeople came from this land of Kham, and the monastery they had built in exile was a modest replica of Khampagar, bearing the same name. Tashi Jong's temple and Institute of Higher Studies, its rituals, art, and masked dances, all evoked their source in that once great center of the Dragon Kargyu lineage of Tibetan Buddhism. The focal point of two hundred branch monasteries and retreat centers, Khampagar had been called the "Glorious Divine Isle of the Wheel of the Law." The refugees' stories and paintings conveyed so vividly its heart-lifting magnificence that it became part of my own interior world, like some Shangri-la which I had known, and for which I too began to yearn.

As our train of ponies carried us westward toward the mountain at whose base it lay, I recalled again the memories of Khampagar that the Tibetans had shared with me. Beyond grand painted gateways and the flutter of prayer flags, curving roofs shone golden through the trees. Around large plazas for processions and lama dances rose libraries, schools, and artists' workshops, their bright walls punctuated with bold colors. Two-story dwellings for the monks, each row with its garden and stable, climbed up the hillside. Higher still, beyond the far-flung monastery walls, hermitages nestled amid rocks and trees.

This was the world to which Bon-pa Tulku, as a newly discovered incarnate lama, was brought at the age of six. This was the world in which he grew up, honored and diligently trained as a scholar, meditator, artist, and administrator. And this was the world he left behind two decades later when, under the pressures of the Chinese occupation, he accompanied Khamtrul Rinpoche, the head of the Dragon Kargyu lineage, into exile. When I knew him in India, I had no idea that political conditions would ever permit his return to Tibet; but now here he was, riding ahead of me in the caravan, taking us with him to Khampagar. On this third trip back, he would settle in for several years to oversee the reconstruction of the temple and the training of new monks.

Slowly the mountain before us grew nearer and daylight began to dim. As our ponies edged around a steep embankment to follow the river northward, the high shoulder above us emitted a thin white column of smoke. Soon I saw a similar smoke-stream rising from the next hillside, and then farther on I glimpsed flame as another was ignited. "They are greeting us," said Lama Kaju smiling, "It is the custom. The fragrance is to please." Monks of Khampagar, their figures indiscernible, burned juniper branches to signal our welcome. No greeting ever stirred me more. Around a third bend in the river, closer figures became visible now, approaching across a low bridge. Coming up to us, they bowed and the white scarves they offered seemed to shine in the dusk. When they took our reins to lead us over the bridge, a strong wild sound filled the valley and echoed between the mountainsides. The long horns of Khampagar were blowing.

It began again to rain, as we were led up from the bridge toward several dozen monks standing amid weeds and rocks. The low, uneven, mud-colored walls behind them were so nondescript that it seemed at first there was nothing there beyond the robed figures and strings sagging with wet prayer flags. The monks, mostly young, greeted us with smiles and stares. The reverence conveyed by the long horns was for the honored tulkus of our party, but the curiosity was for our family of three, the first Westerners ever to come to Khampagar. Eager hands reached to help us dismount and unstrap our gear. Others grasped our arms to lead us through an opening into a yard of liquid mud and guide us across teetering narrow planks. On the far side, we entered the low-ceilinged, candle-lit room that had been prepared for our family.

Store-bought fabric of huge, gaudy red roses covered the walls. Leaning against the walls, were thin beds covered with traditional carpets, and on the floor waited wash basins of hot water. We had reached our destination. We had made it to Khampagar, the Glorious Divine Isle of the Wheel of the Law.

In the privacy of our quarters, we peeled off damp clothes to examine the bruises and chafed places inflicted by the wooden saddles, and luxuriated sparingly with the warm water. We had just finished when we heard a knock on the door and an official visit was announced. In walked Bon-pa Tulku and Abu Nyendrak Rinpoche, offering more white scarves of greeting. They were followed by young monks bearing tea. Formally they greeted us and bade us welcome. Confused by fatigue, it took us a moment to register the fact that these two companions of our journey were appearing now in another role, as presiding officials of the establishment, receiving us into their domain. We had come to a great monastery, and if it was to live again, protocol must be observed. The exquisite etiquette of the Rinpoches was not a denial of the muddy shambles around us, it was a statement of its enduring purpose.

Receiving us graciously, they inquired about any needs we might have for our health and comfort; dinner would be served shortly and tomorrow there would be a tour of the monastery. When we expressed appreciation for our room, the only part of the complex we had seen, they told us its history. After the successive waves of the Chinese Army and then the Red Guards, this storeroom of the old kitchens was the only chamber left intact. It served then as a detention cell for arrested monks before they were driven on foot to distant jails and labor camps. Later on, it functioned as an office for the Chinese government's attempt to organize a collective farm. The attempt was short-lived because many of the local herders disappeared, either dying of starvation when their goods and flocks were expropriated, or leaving to join forces with Khampa resistance fighters. Now, as a more relaxed period of Chinese occupation policy permitted the rebuilding of monasteries and the return of their lamas from exile, it served as the establishment's guest room.

Having heard tales of torture, we inquired further about the sufferings that had been inflicted upon the Tibetans, but Bon-pa Tulku turned our questions aside. As he had demonstrated on earlier occasions, he had little inclination to dwell on the past actions of the Chinese. He was evidently reluctant to express any blame or to arouse it in us.

We were the first Westerners Abu Nyendrak Rinpoche had known, and the round-faced, young abbot, who had never left Tibet, was moved by our visit. He had not accompanied Bon-pa Tulku and the others into exile because he was only seven years old at the time and still lived at home with his family. Being educated and affluent, the entire family was arrested and sentenced to hard labor. "So I am ignorant," he said matter-of-factly, "a Rinpoche never able to study Dharma. I want now to learn the scriptures and do practice but no time now. First it is my duty to build again the monastery." To help pay for supplies and workers' meals, he earns small amounts of money performing the prayers and rituals he knows for villagers and nomads of the region.

Sleep came slowly that night and then, for a long while, only in snatches. I reckoned it was the altitude. I stared into the dark, listening to the wind and the rain and the barking of dogs. I wondered about the monks who had been imprisoned in this room and if any still lived. I wondered if I could find my way to the distant privy we had used, if I needed to go again during the night. I turned gingerly in my sleeping bag and considered ways to fasten a pillow on my saddle for the onward journey.

We were awakened by chanting, cymbals, and drums. The sun was shining. Climbing the ladder near our door to a recently constructed second-story terrace, my husband and I peered into an upper room resounding with loud, eager voices. Lama Kaju, a stocky figure familiar to me from my first days with the refugees back in 1965, and one of the best dancers of Tashi Jong, was sitting with the thirty young monks of Khampagar. His deep tones audible beneath the general exuberance, he led them in the chanted prayers that he had helped preserve in exile.

From the terrace we looked down into the muddy, busy courtyard. Two large hairy beasts, led in by Khampa laymen, waited patiently by the kitchen door with their cargo of fresh red joints of meat. "Yak on yak," said my husband with delight and clicked his camera. Since nearly every dish of every meal in Kham included yak meat, it was just as well that we were not strict vegetarians.

By midmorning we were off on a tour of the monastery complex. Seen in daylight the low, crumbling ruins bore little relation to my fantasies. I was glad to be guided by Bon-pa Tulku himself, for his memories of his twenty-two years of Khampagar life serve as a blueprint for its reconstruction. Exiting from our now familiar courtyard, we reentered the site—"the main South gate stood here." We found ourselves in a vast, drab complex, like a combination construction yard and archaeological dig. Ladders, saw horses, and stacks of fresh-cut lumber were scattered along foundation walls, amidst mounds of ancient masonry. As we walked around them, Bon-pa Tulku pointed to identify: "Here the painters' studios, there the library, over there the monastic college . . . " But in the dun-colored rubble it all looked depressingly the same; my powers of imagination deserted me.

Bon-pa Tulku's pace quickened when he led us across an open space—"This was the main dancing ground"—to a partly scaffolded, multistory edifice where carpenters could be seen at work. With the help of Abu Nyendrak's occasional fees and a small grant from the Chinese government, the central temple was under reconstruction.

The structure for the main prayer hall, built from two partially remaining walls, is spacious, its quadruple rows of high pillars rising to catch the light from windows off upper loggias. On doorways and embrasures, intricate geometric woodwork is already in place, to be painted eventually in bright patterns of color. Bon-pa Tulku pointed to high moldings where brocaded banners will hang and the walls where altars and Buddha figures will be placed. I tried to see the raw, bare hall through his eyes. Familiar with Tibetan monasteries in exile, I could almost imagine it with brocades and painted statues and brass ritual objects glowing in the flickering light shed by banks of butter lamps. We watched Chinese carpenters working a two-man saw. They were hired out of the disbursement received from the provincial government, because they—of the same people who had laid waste to Khampagar—provide a skill no longer available among the local Tibetans. Little Dergen Rinpoche, shyly accompanying us all morning, saw that we were impressed with his playground. Scooping up wood shavings, he tossed them in the air.

As we followed Bon-pa Tulku about, we expressed respect for the work accomplished and the plans in store. But the scale of these plans daunted my heart. With pathetically meager resources, he was acting as if he could restore Khampagar. I was tempted to caution him. I wanted to remind him that his efforts could come to naught, that a change in Chinese policy could reduce his plans to empty dreams. But, of course, he knew that already, far better than I.

Climbing a stairway to the loggia and from there a ladder on up to a roof terrace, he showed us upper chambers designated for special shrine rooms. On that story only a single wall was in place, with windows already mounted in it. Standing on the outer parapet, I looked through them, and instead of an interior saw the green mountains of Kham. I turned my gaze to Bon-pa Tulku himself. We paused there for long moments that are with me still.

That tall, composed figure had been for me a familiar part of Tashi Jong; for years I had seen him moving sedately to execute the social and ritual privileges of his status as an incarnate lama. There he had helped rebuild a Khampagar in exile. There he could be living now in comfort, enjoying the library and the ceremonial functions, and receiving the services of a hundred devoted monks. After the losses and hardships he had known during his flight from Tibet and after all he had done for the refugees, he deserved that ease and security. But now, unquestioningly, as if it were the most natural, logical thing in the world, he was here—in the ruins of his original monastery. With quiet, single-minded persistence, he was undertaking an endeavor that, given the political and economic context, seemed impossible, or foolhardy at best. But perhaps, I reflected, it was no more impossible or foolhardy than the building of Tashi Jong, that vital island of Tibetan culture on Indian soil. Perhaps, for that matter, it was no more unlikely than the creation of Khampagar itself, a wonder of art and learning amidst the rough nomadic peoples of eastern Tibet.

As we stood on the outer wall, I watched Bon-pa Tulku smile calmly as my husband queried him about Chinese policies and the prospects of another period of repression. I saw that such calculations were conjectural to him, as were any guarantees of success. Who knows? And since you cannot know, you simply proceed. You do what you have to do. You put one stone on another and another on top of that. If the stones are knocked down, you begin again, because if you don't, nothing will get built. You persist. Through the vagaries of social events and the seesaw of government policies you persist, because in the long run it is persistence that shapes the future.

Behind the Tulku's demeanor I glimpsed determination and humility combined. He was not afraid of failure. There was too much to restore for the sake of future generations, to let possibilities of failure stay his hand. There was too much at stake to let the past lure him into bitterness. No one had better reason to nurture righteous anger at the Chinese than Bon-pa Tulku and his fellow lamas; but they seemed to have found better uses of the mind.

Two days later we took leave of Khampagar. We had watched how stones were laid and walls of rammed earth erected. We had joined the laypeople who came at sunset to circumambulate the ruins, murmuring prayers. We had walked the hillsides amidst wildflowers, and looked down at the sprawl of mud and masonry, squinting our eyes to imagine golden towers glinting there. Now, climbing on our horses, we prepared to ride south with Nyija and a small party. Abu Nyendrak Rinpoche and little Dergen Rinpoche and Lama Kaju—indeed everyone at Khampagar—assembled to see us off. Bon-pa Tulku stepped forward to bestow white scarves in farewell. From the far side of the bridge, when we turned and waved a last good-bye, his tall figure was still standing calmly by the rubble of the outer walls.

Ten days after our departure from Tibet, an abrupt and brutal reversal occurred in Chinese occupation policy. The more liberal Chinese governor of Tibet was replaced. All movements were restricted and thousands of monks and laypeople, suspected of subversive views, were thrown into prison. The Chinese crackdown, severe in central Tibet, had less effect in Kham.

Reports reached us that the work to restore Khampagar still proceeded. Later on, through the grapevine, word came that it was nearing completion. Whether or not Chinese policies will eventually permit that site to rise again in any semblance of its former grandeur, the persistence of Bon-pa Tulku, Abu Nyendrak and the others may be the real glory of Khampagar.

I don't know if I will see it again. I don't know if I will ever ride again over the green hills of Kham to that company of monks and hear their long horns sound. Present Chinese policy forbids me to travel there; but it cannot block the memory of it. That memory is precious to me, because I know that we too, in our Western world, have to rebuild what has been destroyed.

I don't know where we are going to find the will and stamina to restore our contaminated waters and clear-cut forests, our dying inner cities and the eroded, poisoned soils of our farmlands—if not in the steadiness of heart that I saw in Bon-pa Tulku and in his capacity to let go of blame.

When anger arises over stupid, destructive policies, and the pollution of our world tempts me to hopelessness, I remember his smile on the parapet of Khampagar. And when I catch myself looking for a quick fix, or assurances of success, or simply a mood of optimism before doing what needs to be done, I think of him and hear words that he never spoke.

Don't wait, just do it. A better opportunity may not come along. Place one stone on top of another. Don't waste your spirit trying to compute your short-term chances of success, because you are in it for the long haul. And it will *be* a long haul, with inevitable risks and hardships. So just keep on, steady and spunky like a Khampa pony crossing the mountains, because in the long run, it's our perseverance that counts.

To Reinhabit Time   16

The greater curvature of the universe and of the planet Earth
must govern the curvature of our own being.
—THOMAS BERRY

DEEP ECOLOGY, AND THE group work it inspired, entered my life at about the same time that I became preoccupied with the challenge presented by nuclear waste and its long-term care. By some kind of psychic synergy, these two concerns together invited me to think about time in new ways. I became fascinated by how we, as a culture, relate to time—and what that means for life on Earth. It soon occurred to me that both the progressive destruction of our world, and our capacity to stop that destruction, can be understood as a function of our experience of time.

Let us note, right off, that we of the industrial growth society are subject to a rare and probably unprecedented experience of time. It can be likened to an ever-shrinking box, in which we race on a treadmill at increasingly frenetic speeds. Cutting us off from other rhythms of life, this box cuts us off from the past and future as well. It blocks our perceptual field while allowing only the briefest experience of time.

Until we break out of this temporal trap, we will not be able to fully perceive or adequately address the crises we have created for ourselves and the generations to come. New perspectives have emerged to indicate that we can inhabit time in a healthier, saner fashion. By opening up our experience of time in organic, ecological, and geological terms, we can allow life to continue on Earth.

The Beings of the Three Times

Let us begin as we often do in our workshops for activists—with an invocation of the beings of the three times. We invoke them because, at this historical brink, we need them.

We call first on the beings of the past: Be with us now, all you who have gone before. You, our ancestors and teachers, who walked and loved and faithfully tended this Earth, be present to us now so that we may carry on the legacy you bequeathed us. Aloud and silently in our hearts we say your names and see your faces . . .

We call also on the beings of the present: All you with whom we live and work on this endangered planet, all you with whom we share this brink of time, be with us now. Fellow humans and brothers and sisters of other species, help us open to our collective will and wisdom. Aloud and silently we say your names and picture your faces . . .

Lastly we call on the beings of the future: All you who will come after us on this Earth, be with us now. All you who are waiting to be born in the ages to come, it is for your sakes too that we work to heal our world. We cannot picture your faces or say your names—you have none yet—but we feel the reality of your claim on life. It helps us to be faithful in the task that must be done, so that there will be for you, as there was for our ancestors: blue sky, fruitful land, clear waters.

The Reading of the Will

In contrast to this prayer, our true regard for the beings of the future is closer to that portrayed by cartoonist Tom Toles. To a group sitting before him expectantly, a lawyer is reading a will. It says:

Dear Kids,

We, the generation in power since World War II, seem to have used up pretty much everything ourselves. We kind of drained all the resources out of our manufacturing industries, so there's not much left there. The beautiful old buildings that were built to last for centuries, we tore down and replaced with character-less but inexpensive structures, and you can have them. Except everything we built has a life span about the same as ours, so, like the interstate highway system we built, they're all falling apart now and you'll have to deal with that. We used up as much of our natural resources as we could, without providing for renewable ones, so you're probably only good until about a week from Thursday. We did build a generous Social Security and pension system, but that was just for us. In fact, the only really durable thing we built was toxic dumps. You can have those. So think of your inheritance as a challenge. The challenge of starting from scratch. You can begin as soon as—oh, one last thing—as soon as you pay off the two trillion dollar debt we left you.

Signed, Your Parents

What is staggering about this cartoon, to the point of being funny, is not any exaggeration, for there is none, but the sheer enormity of the reality it portrays and our blithe acceptance of it. Our national deficit of nearly 9 trillion dollars, for example, has more than quadrupled in the twenty-two years since Toles's cartoon. This state of affairs can be approached, of course, from a moralistic perspective, in terms of the selfishness of our generation. But I find it more helpful to understand it in terms of our experience of time; for it reveals a pathetically shrunken sense of time and a pathological denial of its continuity.

This disregard for the future is all the more astonishing since it runs counter to our nature as biological systems. Living organisms are built to propagate, and to invest a great deal of time and energy in the complex set of behaviors that effort requires. Through these behaviors, which usually have no direct survival value to the individual, the future is wired in. There is, as systems-thinker Tyrone Cashman points out, "this spilling out into the future that is the entire essence of organisms. Any plant or animal for whom, throughout its species history, this was not its most essential characteristic would not exist at all. This wired-in relationship to time is alterable only at the price of extinction. Of course, this time-thrust, this into-the-future-ness of all living beings can be lost by a species. But then, immediately, the species itself disappears, forever."

The Broken Connection

This systems design common to all organisms is clearly evident throughout human history. At great personal cost men and women have labored to create monuments of art and learning that would endure far beyond their individual lives. It makes our present generation's disregard for the future appear amazing, indeed. What developments can account for it?

For one thing, the atomic bomb has happened. The advent of nuclear weapons has ruptured our sense of biological continuity and our felt connections with both past and future. Arguing this point, Robert J. Lifton says, "We need not enter the debate as to whether nuclear war would or would not eliminate *all* human life. The fact that there is such a debate in itself confirms the importance of *imagery* of total biological destruction, or radically impaired imagination of human continuity." This impairment reaches backward as well as forward, "since our sense of connection with prior generations . . . depends on feeling part of a continuing sequence of generations. The image of a destructive force of unlimited dimensions . . . enters into every relationship involving parents, children, grandparents, and imagined great-grandparents and great-grandchildren. . . . We are thus among the first to live with a recurrent sense of biological severance."

From the thousands of people I've met in workshops, I know this to be true. When people feel safe to express their inner responses to the nuclear and the ecological crises, it is the threats to all life that surface as their deepest and most pervasive anguish. This anguish is far greater than fears for their individual well-being.

The Future Canceled

The sense of biological severance, to which Lifton attests, finds form and reinforcement in corporate and governmental policies, which continue to embody the frontier mentality that came to the fore in the Reagan administration. This mentality denies any need to steward the Earth for the sake of the future, because there would always be fresh, unlimited land to move on to. Tyrone Cashman explains the connection:

> When the frontier was over, when there was no more empty land, no more unexplored territory, the engine of American ambition had no place to go. What we have done, and elected Ronald Reagan to stand as symbol for, is to cancel the future.
>
> Reagan essentially assured us, through his personal lack of concern for the future, his escalation of nuclear weapons production, and his own public comments about Armageddon and the end of history, that the future was canceled, that we needn't concern ourselves about it anymore. Thus, it became morally permissible to treat the lands we live on and the rivers and the soils and the forests much as we had treated them when we knew there was an unlimited open

frontier in the West for us to move to when the lands we were exploiting were exhausted, destroyed, and befouled.

When the future is canceled, there is no need to care for the lands we live on. As former Secretary of Interior James Watt so clearly stated, we can use it all up now because we are the last generation. The great feeding frenzy of the 1980s—when the economy was partly deregulated and leveraged buyouts and hostile takeovers were a daily occurrence—resulted in part from a sense of the end of an era. And those who had the power to salt the stuff away before the whole thing went to hell were out to do just that.

The Time Squeeze

These developments are aggravated by a lifestyle of increasing speed. We suffer ever more chronically from the loss not only of past and future, but of the present as well. We hurry. We complain about crowded schedules and the pressure of commitments, then check our watches and rush on. We experience burnout and work hard to earn moments where life can cease and we can relax—then take our laptop computer along on vacation.

Time itself, both as a commodity and an experience, has become a scarcity. It is a painful irony that we who have more time-saving devices than any culture in any period appear the most time-harried and driven. The paradox is only apparent, however, for our time-scarcity is linked to the very time-efficiency of our technology. As Jeremy Rifkin chronicles in *Time Wars,* our measure of time that once was based on the changing seasons and wheeling stars, and then with the ticking of the clock, is now parceled out in computer nanoseconds— we have lost time as an organically measurable experience.

The hurry in which we live invades our thought processes, our bodies, and our relationships. As Alfred Herehausen, former board chair of the Deutsche Bank, reflected, "We suffer from a remarkable illness, a hectic fever. We don't take time to ponder things, to think them through to the end."

Larry Dossey, physician and author of *Space, Time and Medicine,* points out that this causes "hurry sickness." "Our perceptions of speeding clocks and vanishing time cause our own biological clocks to speed. The end result is frequently some form of hurry sickness—expressed as heart disease, high blood pressure, or depression of our immune function, leading to an increased susceptibility to infection and cancer."

We find ourselves moving too fast for the cultivation of friendships and cross-cultural solidarity, which have their own tempo. Self-disclosure and the unfolding of trust are not always time-efficient and time-predictable. In the classroom, even the age-old relationship between student and teacher suffers. "My teachers talk slower than my computer," complains a nine-year-old, "so slow they make me mad sometimes. I think, 'Come on, enough of this, let me go home to my computer. It tells me things faster.'"

The *Kali Yuga*—the "age of iron"—is ancient India's name for the final degenerative era of a world cycle. One meaning of Kali Yuga is "the dregs of time." We experience a temporal density, gritty and bitter as used coffee grounds. In this final stage, time gets extreme, speeds up, clogs our pores.

My second trip to see my son on a wilderness farm in northern British Columbia was only one year after the first visit. As I trekked the last part of the twenty-five miles from the nearest public road, I looked up at the surrounding mountains and saw changes so startling they stopped me in my tracks. The once beautiful, wild slopes and ridges of cedar and Douglas fir were now defaced by huge square areas—clear-cut, unsightly. "Pampers," said my son, when I asked who had done the damage, "it's a company that makes paper diapers."

All week, as I helped with the haying and the milking of the goats, I would look up at those mountainsides in anger and grief. "I never put paper diaperes on *my* children," I muttered. Actually they were not mass produced then, so I soaked and washed cloth ones as my mother had before me. To be honest, I have to admit that if I were a young mother today I'd be tempted to use the disposable ones, because, of course, I would be in a hurry. Because we are forced to rush, and because we are so disconnected from the results of our action, we cut down an old-growth forest and dump more tons of waste in our landfills to save ourselves ten or fifteen minutes.

Speed and haste, as many a wise one has pointed out, are inherently violent. The violence they inflict on our environment is not only because of our appetite for time-saving devices and materials, but also because they put us out of sync with the ecosystem. The natural systems that sustain us move at slower rhythms than we do. The feedback loop is longer, takes more time than our interactions with machines. We are like the hummingbird that has such a high metabolic rate it can't see the movements of the bear coming slowly out of hibernation. To the bird, the bear appears as stationary as a glacier does to us. Our own accelerating speed puts us out of sync with more and more of the natural world and blinds us to our impact upon it.

By speed we strive to conquer time. It doesn't take much subtlety to see how this catches us in a vicious circle. The time-pressures we create in our computerized world further inflame our desire to escape from time. In cybernetic terms, this is a classic positive feedback loop—and we are all victims of it. No matter how we writhe and turn to free ourselves from time, we twist ourselves more tightly in it. We become enslaved by what we would master, devoured by what we would consume, and increasingly view it—yes, view time itself—as the enemy.

Spirituality as Escape from Time

Increasing numbers of us turn to spiritual practices, such as meditation, to find release from this rat race. Closing our eyes, breathing deeply and slowly, we seek to rise above the pressures of our days into a timeless calm. This behavior can be helpful in slowing us down a bit, but it often perpetuates the notion of time as an enemy to be conquered or outwitted.

In classical Hindu thought, time is considered to be unreal, a trap of illusion, a form of maya from which to escape into the more ultimate reality of timelessness. In Buddhism more reality is accorded to time and change; yet Buddhist teachers often use the teaching of impermanence to point to the unsatisfactoriness of life, as a prod to meditative practice. What you cherish soon passes. Flowers wilt, paint peels, lovers leave, your own body sags, wrinkles, and decays. Ah, woe! Better fix your gaze on what is free from the ravages of time.

Western religions as well reveal this animosity to time. Reach for eternity. Keep your eyes on the pie in the sky. New Age spiritualities with their oft-repeated injunctions to "Be Here Now" can also serve to devalue chronological time and encourage disregard for the future.

This mindset among people of different religious backgrounds was evident at a gathering I called to reflect on our experience of time. Everyone spoke feelingly about the frenzied and fragmented pace of daily life. When I invited them to hypothesize alternatives to these pressures, only one alternative was suggested: escape into timelessness. The only remedy they saw was to cultivate an experience of eternity aloof from chronological time.

This bothered me a lot, because I was working hard on the issue of nuclear waste. I was looking for ways to relate to time that could help us face up to the challenge of their incredibly long-lived radioactivity. I wanted us to find the ability to inhabit time in longer stretches, not escape from it altogether.

It occurred to me then that our fear of time is, like our fear of matter, a legacy of the patriarchal mindset. This essentially dualistic mindset has tended to view the spiritual journey as an attempt to extricate spirit from the toils of matter. Has this mentality devalued chronological time in the same manner? Can we not see an equation here? The formula would be this: As spirit is to matter, so eternity is to time. Each side of the equation sets that which we seek to escape *to* in relation to that which we seek to escape *from*.

$$\frac{\text{SPIRIT}}{\text{MATTER}} = \frac{\text{ETERNITY}}{\text{TIME}}$$

This equation triggers other reflections. By setting it in opposition to eternity, we have come to perceive time as an enemy. We strive to conquer it. And now, thanks to our technology, we are in great danger of succeeding. A key feature of our nuclear war-making capacity is speed. The technological design thrust is to accelerate response to attack, and make launch-on-warning as instantaneous as possible. The time allowed for human appraisal and intervention—to see, for example, if the attack is real or the result of a computer misreading—is continually reduced. Our nuclear missiles may be the logical unfolding of our "spiritual" desire to escape from time. So let us ask, how can we move beyond our fear of time so that our days on Earth may be long?

Reclaiming Story

To fall in love again with time, we need narrative. "It's all a question of story," says Thomas Berry. "We are in trouble just now because we do not have a good story." Though they hold little meaning for us now, we had some good stories of our world in the past. "They did not necessarily make people good, nor did they take away the pains and stupidities of life or make for unfailing warmth in human association. They did provide a context in which life could function in a meaningful manner." And that is all we ask right now, that life function in a meaningful manner—or just function, period.

Berry and his colleague, cosmologist Brian Swimme, hold that the new story we need to guide us through the perils of this era must include the whole universe and all its beings. Only in that context can we perceive the long panorama and web of kinship that is basic to the magnitude of the commitment we are called now to make. Story nourishes, as they point out, a "time-developmental consciousness."

And our particular story, Earth's and ours, has, of necessity, both grandeur and pain.

Perhaps only by seeing the permanent destruction we have inflicted upon the Earth Community can we come to the realization that the Earth Community is in fact a dimension of ourselves. Perhaps only when that loss is felt personally, can the human realize the grandeur of the human in the grandeur of the Earth. Perhaps only by feeling directly the folly of destroying Earth's beauty can we awaken to the simple truth that we are destroying our macrophase self.

To appropriate the story of evolving Earth as our own can radically expand our consciousness of time and our felt continuity with past and future. In the Work That Reconnects we set about this deliberately and experientially. We engage, for example in ancestral and evolutionary "rememberings," expanding our time frame to include the story of our species or the life span of our planet. Our purpose is to deepen our sense of what is personally at stake for us in global issues, and also to strengthen our sense of authority when we act in defense of life. We act then not from the private whim or personal nobility of our short-lived individual ego, but clothed in the full authority of our four and a half billion years.

Our Life as Gaia

This guided meditation offers an opportunity to re-story our identity as Gaia. It is done with a group and a drum. It can also, of course, be done alone in stillness or interwoven with our daily activities.

Come back into a story we all share, a story whose rhythm beats in us still. The story belongs to each of us and to all of us, like the beat of this drum, like the heartbeat of our living universe.

There is science now to construct the story of the journey we have made on this Earth, connecting us with all beings. There is great yearning and great need to own that story—to break out of our isolation and recover our larger identity. The challenge to do that now is perhaps the most wonderful aspect of being alive today. It can give us the courage and high spirits to dance our people into sanity and solidarity. Let us remember it together.

With the heartbeat of the drum we hear the rhythm that has accompanied us all the way and underlies all our days and doings. So let it take us back now through our lives, back through our childhood, back through our birth. In our mother's womb there was that same sound, that same beat, as we floated in the fluid right under her heart.

Let that beat take us back farther still. Let's go back beyond our conception, back to the first splitting and spinning of the stars. As scientists measure now, it is fourteen billion years ago we manifested as a universe—in the primal flaring forth.

There we were, careening out with the speed of light, creating space and time. We were great swirling clouds of gas—can you remember? And the particles, as they circled in the dance, desired each other and formed atoms.

Ten billion years later, one of those swirling masses split off from its blazing sun—the sun we feel now on our faces. And our lifetime as Gaia began.

Touch our Earth. Touch your face, that is Gaia, too.

In the immediate planet-time of ours, Gaia is becoming aware of herself—through us.

Let us imagine that our life as a planet could be condensed into twenty-four hours, beginning at midnight. Until five o'clock the following afternoon all her adventures are geological. All was volcanic flame and steaming rains washing over the shifting bones of the continents into the seas—only at five o'clock comes organic life.

To the heartbeat of life in you and this drum, you, too, can shift free from identifying solely with your latest, human, form. The fire of those early volcanoes, the strength of those tectonic plates, is in us still. For in our very bodies, we carry traces of Gaia's story as organic life. We were aquatic first, as we remember in our mother's womb, growing vestigial gills and fins. The salt from those early seas flows still in our sweat and tears. The age of the dinosaurs we carry with us, too, in our reptilian brain, right at the end of our spinal column. Complex organic life learned to protect itself and it is all there in our instinct to flee or fight.

When did we appear as mammals? In those twenty-four hours of Gaia's life, it was at 11:30 PM. When did we become human? One second to midnight.

Now let us take that second to midnight that is our story as humans and render it, in turn, into twenty-four hours. Let's look back through the twenty-four hours that we have been human.

Beginning at midnight and until two o'clock in the afternoon, we live in small groups in Africa. Can you remember? We feel pretty vulnerable; we haven't the speed of the other creatures, or their claws or fangs or natural armor. But we have our remarkable hands, opposable thumbs to help shape tools and weapons. We have in our throats and frontal lobes the capacity for speech. And we have each other. Grunts and calls turn into language as we collaborate in strategies and rituals. Those days and nights on the verge of the forests, as we weave baskets and stories around our fires, represent the longest chapter of our human experience.

Then in small bands we begin branching out. We move across the face of Gaia; we learn to endure the cold and hunt the mammoth and name the trees of the northern forest, the flowers and seasons of the tundra. We know it is Gaia by whom we live. We make carvings of her with breasts and hips to worship her life-giving abundance.

When we settle into agriculture, when we begin domesticating animals and fencing off our croplands and deciding that they can be owned as private property, when we build great cities with granaries and temples and observatories to chart the stars, the time is 11:58. Two minutes to midnight.

At 11:59 comes a time of quickening change. We want to chart the stars within as well as those we see in the skies. We seek the authority of inner experience. To free the questing mind we set it apart from Gaia. We make conjectures and rules and heroes to chart our freedom to think and act. At six seconds to midnight appear the Buddha and Lao-tzu and right on their heels come Jesus of Nazareth, Mohammed, and the Great Peacemaker of the Haudenosaunee.

What now shapes our world—our industrial society with its factories, bombs and bulldozers—has arisen in the last few microseconds of our day as humans. Yet those few microseconds bring us right to the brink of time. For the forces our technologies have unleashed, and the power they give to our fears and greed, threaten all life.

We are now at a point unlike any other in our story. Perhaps we have, in some way, chosen to be here at this culminating chapter or turning point. We have opted to be alive when the stakes are high, to test everything we have ever learned about interconnectedness and courage—to test it now when it could be the end of conscious life on this beautiful water planet hanging like a jewel in space.

In primal societies rites of passage are held for adolescents, because it is then that the fact of personal death or mortality is integrated into the personality. The individual goes through the prescribed ordeal of the initiation rite in order to integrate that knowledge, so that he or she can assume the rights and responsibilities of adulthood. That is what we are doing right now on the collective level in this planet-time. We are confronting and integrating into our awareness our mortality as a species. We must do that so that we can wake up and assume the rights and responsibilities of planetary adulthood. That is, in a sense, what we are doing here.

When you go out from here, keep listening to the drumbeat. You will hear it in your heart. And as you hear it, remember that it is the heartbeat of the universe as well, your larger Self.

When you return to your communities to organize, saying no to the machinery of death and yes to life, remember your true identity. Remember our story. Clothe yourself in your authority. You were not born yesterday. You know in your heartbeat and bones the precarious, exquisite balance of life. Out of that knowledge you can speak and act, not only for yourself. You will speak and act with the courage and endurance that has been yours through the long, beautiful eons of your life story as Gaia.

Bridge to the Far Future

While the use of imagination to remember our evolution and reconnect with our ancestors can expand our awareness of the past, analogous practices can make the future more real. Ecological restoration work brings a strong connection with coming generations. To plant a tree extends one's sense of tenure on this Earth. Careful, compelling novels like *Always Coming Home* by Ursula LeGuin or *Spirit Walker* by Hank Wesselman, can inspire a bond with far distant generations and help us respect their claim on life.

Nuclear wastes can serve as a bridge to the far future, because it extends the effects of our actions—our karma—into the thousands and even millions of years that their hazardous life entails.

The way we and other countries have produced and disposed of these materials ranks among the most appalling displays of our denial of the future. Radioactivity produces not only disease, death, and sterility, it affects the genetic code itself. Likened to a madman in a library, it can scramble and lose forever the blueprints for life crafted by our long evolutionary journey. Yet, knowing this, we dump millions of metric tons of this waste into open trenches, into the sea, into cardboard boxes, into tanks that crack and corrode within a decade or two.

The only final solution for high level waste that our government can come up with is to hide it, out of sight and out of mind, in deep geological repositories—although this strategy makes leaking containers inaccessible for repair. Seeking to generate alternative responses to nuclear waste, I have experimented with ways that would help people experience, on a gut level, its ongoingness through time. On one occasion at an ad hoc "People's Council" in New Mexico, when discussion about the waste was limited to wishing it away, I pulled out a small tape recorder. "Let's imagine," I said, "that if we can't stop the waste from going into the Carlsbad repository, we can at least place this cassette there on the surface for future generations to find and listen to. What do we want to say to them?"

Passing the recorder among them, the men and women began to speak into it. "My name is George, I'm back in the late twentieth century and I'm trying to stop them from burying this radioactive waste. If you find this and you can hear this, listen. This stuff is dangerous! Don't dig here. It's deadly, take care."

As the words came, the distant, unborn ones to whom they were addressed became more and more real to us. We began to inhabit large stretches of time. Understanding arose that the wastes should be kept in visible, reparable, ground-level storage; and several young people volunteered to live and work at such a "Guardian Site."

Our radioactive legacy has had another peculiar effect on my experience of time. Suffering from the big squeeze as much as anyone, time's main meaning for me was scarcity and haste. Especially in social action, the clock was always ticking. Hurry, hurry to stop the next development project in the Amazon, the construction of yet another youth prison, or the next arms shipment to Iraq. Make those calls, circulate those petitions, hurry to keep the world from blowing up or heating up; the countdown is on. When the longevity of nuclear toxicity dawned on me, I glimpsed what this challenge would mean in terms of sustained human attention and the demands of time reversed themselves. The question of how fast one could get something done was replaced with the question of how long—how *lo-o-n-n-ng*—a period one could do it in. Will we actually be able to remember the danger of these wastes and protect ourselves for a hundred years, a thousand, or a hundred thousand? As I pondered the likelihood of this, the challenge became duration not speed; the long haul, not the quick move. My breath slowed, the rib cage eased. The horror of the waste was helping me inhabit time.

The Seventh Generation

We have the ability, through our moral imagination, to break out of our temporal confine and let longer expanses of time become real to us. We can do it and even be good at it. The exercise called the Double Circle, or "The Seventh Generation," lets us experience ourselves as ancestors and see our lives through the eyes of future beings.

People sit in two concentric circles that are of the same size and face each other, so that there is always someone directly in front of them. Those in the outer circle speak for themselves, from their own experience; those in the inner circle are of seven generations from now, or about 200 years. We imagine that the encounter between them occurs "at a point outside of time."

Before it begins, the facilitator explains that the process rests on two assumptions, which she asks the participants to grant. The first is that humans exist two centuries from now. For the purpose of this exercise, we do not need to know how many or in what state of health or comfort they live, but we grant their existence. The second assumption is that these humans know about what happened in our time, which means they have institutions capable of carrying an unbroken cultural memory. And *that* means they live in a sustainable society, and the Great Turning has happened. For the industrial growth system, already spinning out of control, cannot last many more decades, let alone two centuries.

Once instructions for their interchanges are completed, the group's journey to a point outside of time is marked by their chanting a sustained "ah," the seed syllable evoking those who have no voice.

Each of the three encounters is initiated by a query *to* the present-day person *from* the future being. It is imagined that this query is made telepathically, heart to heart, although it is *heard* in the voice of the facilitator. The present-day ones respond by speaking to the future being directly in front of them, continuing for several minutes. The facilitator signals when it is time to conclude, provides a brief silence, then asks the future beings to all move one seat to the right. The new partners exchange a silent greeting and the facilitator gives the next question.

The three questions, which the guide speaks on behalf of the future ones, are given here in words we *tend* to use.

1   Ancestor, I greet you. Our teachers tell us things about your time that I find hard to believe. They say bombs were still being made that could destroy whole cities. They say there were some people richer than the richest ancient kings, and billions of people without shelter and clean water and enough to eat. They say whole species of plants and animals were going extinct—ah, we know about that!—but they tell us that you knew it too while it was happening. Tell me, is all this really true? And if it *is*, then what is it like for you to live in such a world?

2   Ancestor, we still have songs and stories that tell of what you and your friends are doing for the Great Turning. Now what I want to know is this: how did you start? When did you first realize that the industrial growth society was doomed? You must have felt lonely and confused sometimes, especially at the beginning. What first steps did you take?

3   Ancestor, I know you didn't stop with those first actions on behalf of Earth. Tell me, where do you find the strength and joy to continue working so hard, despite all the obstacles and discouragements?

When the last question has been answered, the future ones do not move on, but stay where they are. Now it is their turn to talk, while the present-day person listens. They speak what is in their hearts after all they have just heard from their ancestors. What often comes is deep and surprising, so we give it time and then the pairs close with silent affirmations of respect. To reenter ordinary time, where the future ones' roles are released, the group sounds ah again, as at the beginning; this provides a firm ritual closing.

Politics of Time

If, for a livable world, we must learn to reinhabit time, what changes are required in our system of self-governance? What political practices would reflect and encourage a sense of responsibility to coming generations? Such questions prompt a wide range of proposals. Extending the terms of legislative office would relieve representatives from the pressures of constant electoral campaigns and allow them time to think. Alterations in executive budgetary requirements would free disbursements from having to be hastily made in a given fiscal year.

Let's create structures that would give voice to the interests of future generations. This is totally in keeping with our principle of no taxation without representation. Since we are taxing future generations by the exploitation of their resources, they should have their say in the process. Because they are not born yet, or too young to vote, offices should be instituted where pronouncements can be made on their behalf.

One possibility has a precedent in the Congressional offices of representatives of Puerto Rico and the District of Columbia. Though without a legislative vote, they are provided the means to bring views and needs of their constituencies to the attention of Congress. I propose a similar nonvoting representative for the people of the future, to promote their needs and bring a larger perspective on time into legislative debates. This representative could be selected at a special three-day convention in Washington, which would in itself be a salutary exercise in raising awareness of the effects of our present policies on coming generations.

A second possibility has even greater potential for changing our society's consciousness of time. Consider the establishment of a third house of Congress, a House of Spokespersons for the Future. Though without the power to pass laws, it would speak for the rights of coming generations. Its members, or "Spokes," would be high school seniors, two from each state, chosen at statewide conventions on Congressional election years. The House of Spokes would convene in Washington for a week three times a year, evaluate bills before Congress and suggest new legislation. During the balance of the year its members would still be heard from, as they point to the priorities they see appropriate for a healthy and decent future.

Our relation to time shapes our goals and values. Recognition of this fact suggests a reconceptualization of the political spectrum—from spatial to temporal terms. Jeremy Rifkin suggests that political persuasions and loyalties formerly assigned to categories of "right" and "left" will sort themselves out more accurately and usefully in terms of their orientation to rhythms and duration of time. A more useful and realistic political spectrum would reflect differences between short-term and long-term thinking. The latter would reintegrate our social and economic pace with the tempos of the natural world so that the ecosystem can "heal itself and become a vibrant, living organism once again."

Since we as a species have no future apart from the health of that organism, this return to a more organic, ecological experience of time is a matter of survival. And we don't need to wait until we have created new institutions. We can begin now; through our choices and mindfulness. We can watch time's rhythm in the breathing of the moment, and sense how its very passage connects us with the past and future moments. They become to us like unseen guides and companions as we once again reinhabit time.

In League with the Beings of the Future

17

For thou shalt be in league with the stones of the field,
and the beasts of the field shall be at peace with thee.
—JOB 5:23

THIS VERSE OF THE Bible delighted me as a child and stayed with me as I grew up. It promised a way I wanted to live—in complicity with creation. It still comes to mind when I hear about people taking action on behalf of other species. When our brothers and sisters of Greenpeace or Earth First! put their lives on the line to save marine mammals or the old-growth forests, I think, "Ah, they're in league."

To be "in league" in that way seems wonderful. There is a comfortable, cosmic collegiality to it—like coming home to conspire once more with our beloved and age-old companions, with the stones and the beasts of the field, with the sun that rises and the stars revolving in the sky.

Now the work of restoring our ravaged Earth offers us that—with a new dimension. It not only puts us in league with the stones and the beasts, but also in league with the beings of the future. All that we do to mend our planet is for their sake, too. Their chance to live and love our world depends in large measure on us and our uncertain efforts.

The Presence of the Future

"Every being who will ever live in Earth is here right now," says Sister Rosalie Bertell, environmental health radiologist and leader of the Bhopal and Chernobyl Medical Commissions. "Where? In our gonads and ovaries, and in our DNA."

The beings of the future and their claim on life have come to seem so real to me that I sense them hovering, like a cloud of witnesses. Sometimes I fancy that if I were to turn my head suddenly, I would glimpse them over my shoulder. Philosophers and mystics say that chronological time is a construct, a function of our mentality; there is also, they say, a dimension in which all time is simultaneous, where we coexist with past and future. Perhaps because I am so time-ridden, hurrying to meet this deadline and that appointment, I am drawn to that notion. The dimension of simultaneity, where we stand shoulder to shoulder with our ancestors and posterity, is appealing to me, giving context and fuel to work for social change.

In that context it is plausible to me that the generations of the future want to lend us courage for what we do. I imagine them saying "thank you" for our efforts to keep mines from leaching into rivers and topsoil from blowing away. Thanks for our citizen campaigns on behalf of the sea. Thank you, ancestors, for working on renewable energy sources, so that we may have some clean air to breathe.

The imagined presence of these future ones comes to me like grace and works upon my life. They are why I have been drawn, almost despite myself, to the distasteful issue of radioactive waste. In terms of time and toxicity, it's the most enduring legacy our generation will leave behind.

Awakened by Dreams

To many of us, dreams are coming that portray frightening scenes of the future. We rise from bed still haunted by images of tidal waves, wasted landscapes, and social chaos. It is important to remember that these nightmares arise from the collective psyche, warning us of dangers we often ignore in our waking lives. They are not a prediction so much as a summons. They challenge us to incorporate their content into conscious awareness and free them from the grip of unconscious forces. As Carl Gustav Jung explained, if we repress subliminal fears intimated in our dreams, they are more likely to be acted out on the stage of history.

In the late 1970s, I had such a dream. At the time, I was taking part in a citizens' lawsuit to stop faulty storage of high-level waste at a nearby nuclear reactor. My job was to review and summarize public health statistics in order to substantiate our legal claims. I poured over research revealing mounting incidence of miscarriages, birth defects, leukemia and other cancers in the proximity of nuclear plants. Learning that genetic damage would compound over time, I strained to conceive of *spans* of time like a quarter million years, the hazardous life of plutonium. One night, before going to bed, I had leafed through baby pictures of our three children to find a snapshot for my daughter's high school yearbook.

In the dream I behold the three of them as they appeared in the old photos, and am struck most by the sweet wholesomeness of their flesh. My husband and I are journeying with them across an unfamiliar landscape. The terrain becomes dreary, treeless and strewn with rocks; little Peggy can barely clamber over the boulders in the path. Just as the going is getting very difficult, even frightening, I suddenly realize that by some thoughtless but unalterable prearrangement, their father and I must leave them. I can see the grimness of the way that lies ahead for them, bleak as a red moonscape and with a flesh-burning sickness in the air. I am maddened by sorrow that my children must face this without me. I kiss each one and tell them we will meet again, but I know no place to name where we will meet. Perhaps another planet, I say. Innocent of terror, they try to reassure me, ready to be off. Removed, and from a height in the sky, I watch them go—three small solitary figures trudging across that angry wasteland, holding each other by the hand and not stopping to look back. In spite of the widening distance, I see with a surrealist's precision the ulcerating of their flesh. I see how the skin bubbles and curls back to expose raw tissue as they doggedly go forward, the boys helping their little sister across the rocks.

I woke up, brushed my teeth, showered, and tried to wash those images away. But when I roused Peggy for school, I sank beside her bed. "Hold me," I said, "I had a bad dream." With my face in her warm nightie, inhaling her fragrance, I found myself sobbing. I sobbed against her body, against her seventeen-year-old womb, as the knowledge of all that assails it surfaced in me. The statistical studies on the effects of ionizing radiation, the dry columns of figures, their import beyond utterance, turned now to wracking tears.

Our citizens' group lost its suit against the Virginia Electric Power Company, but it taught me a lot. It taught me that all children for centuries to come are my children. It taught me about the misuse of our technology and the obscenity of the legacy it bequeaths future generations—lessons confirmed over and over again by exposes of mismanagement, accidents, and spills at nuclear installations. "Temporarily" stored in pools and corrodible containers, they leak into air, soil, aquifers, and rivers, as confirmed in at least thirty-four of the United States, while the only long-term solution contrived by government and industry is deep burial in the ground, which makes it impossible to monitor and repair the containers.

The Poison Fire as Teacher

From the perspective of future generations, this policy—to put the waste out of sight and out of mind—amounts to betrayal. As we discover in other aspects of our lives, hiding doesn't work in the long run. This is especially true of nuclear materials because, irradiated by their contents, containers corrode. As Earth's strata shift and water seeps, the radioactivity spreads—into the aquifers, into the biosphere, into lungs and wombs. Already, from the one operating repository in Carlsbad, New Mexico, contaminated salt brine is leaking through underground fissures to the Pecos River on its way to the Gulf of Mexico.

I remember visiting this repository during its construction. When I asked the Westinghouse engineers how future generations would be protected from contamination, they said the site would be safe for a good hundred years. "And after that?" I asked. They look at me blankly, as if puzzled by such a strange question.

Standing there in the briefing room, I wondered how that question would be answered if we inhabited Earth with a realistic sense of time. If we felt the aliveness of our planet home and connection with those who come after, would we still want to sweep these wastes under the rug, hide them like a secret shame, and go on about our business as before?

A different approach to nuclear waste had occurred to me in Great Britain in the early 1980s when I visited Greenham Common and other citizen encampments surrounding U.S. nuclear missile bases. I sensed immediately their commitment to the future. With their unflagging dedication and strong spiritual flavor, these encampments called to mind the monasteries that kept the lamp of learning alive through the Dark Ages. I realized then that communities with similar dedication will be needed to guard the centers of radioactivity we are bequeathing to tens of thousands of future generations.

In my mind's eye I could see surveillance communities forming around today's nuclear facilities. I imagined I saw Guardian Sites—centers of reflection and pilgrimage, where the waste containers are monitored and repaired, and where wisdom traditions of our planetary heritage offer contexts of meaning and disciplines of vigilance. Here "remembering" would be undertaken—the crucial task of understanding the origins and nature of this radioactivity, as well as ongoing mindfulness of its danger. Here those who come for varying periods of time participate in an active learning community—to receive training and take their turn at nuclear guardianship.

The vision stayed with me. Recruiting colleagues, I formed a study-action group on nuclear waste, to comprehend the dangers in current practices and the requirements for responsible long-term care.

Similar groups formed in other countries. Desiring throughout to be "in league with the beings of the future," we invited them to our sessions through evocations and prayerful listening, scenario games and role-plays. We began to use the future ones' name for our radioactive legacy: "the poison fire." We first heard it in our simulation games when we would speak on behalf of generations to come. The term immediately struck a chord because it pierces through the techno-speak and bureaucratic jargon that often obscures the issue. It also suggests a power that is both sacred and dangerous.

Our study-action group soon addressed the wider public in an educational endeavor called the Nuclear Guardianship Project. To promote on-site, retrievable storage of nuclear waste, we published a free tabloid and testified at regulatory hearings. We also presented to churches, schools, and any organization that invited us. As I recall some of those many presentations, I am awed by their creative audacity, as they conveyed—with music, projected images, and enactments—the perspective and needs of future generations.

We wanted the future ones to become as real to others as they were to us. We wanted to share the teachings we had received from them:

> You, in whose generation the poison fire was made, you have some obligations. You need technical training in radiation and protection from it. You need moral training, as well, in the vigilance required to keep it out of the biosphere. No containment lasts as long as the poison fire itself. You cannot hide it and walk away. But so long as you pay attention, so long as it's kept visible to the watchful eye and accessible for repair, you will be guardians—and you will pass that learning on to us. To carry that responsibility through the chaos to come, faithful commitment is essential—and community to sustain it. So begin now.

Becoming Guardians

This call is being heeded, not just in specific sites of contamination, but as a principle to uphold in every aspect of our lives. Take the Precautionary Principle and see how fast it has entered public discourse and policy. Developed by scientists and lawyers in the Science and Environmental Health Network (SEHN), the Precautionary Principle draws on the German concept of *Vorsorge,* or forecare, to serve as an economic and legal framework that takes into account the potential harm of any human activity. Carolyn Raffensperger, one of SEHN's founding visionaries, calls it plain common sense or the grandmother principle: "better safe than sorry," "an ounce of prevention is worth a pound of cure," "a stitch in time saves nine." It reverses the burden of proof from those who may be harmed to those who propose new development and technologies—be they untested chemicals, genetically-modified organisms, or the siting of industrial plants. The Precautionary Principle requires us to explore the range of safe alternatives, including no action at all.

Terry Tempest Williams defines this concept as "restraint in the name of reverence." It is an idea whose time has come. San Francisco has passed it as a county-wide ordinance; the Florida and Hawaii constitutions have incorporated it into their environmental policies; a growing number of hospitals and schools are choosing to bring healthy alternatives into daily choices and practices.

Now the Guardianship Project has emerged as a cultural expression of the Precautionary Principle. It invites individuals, neighborhoods, or any kind of organization to voluntarily assume responsibility for one strand in the web of life, be it the stream at the edge of your block, a species of bird you love, or a language in danger of dying out. As the Project enlists us in learning about and protecting our chosen life form, our passion is put into service. Shepherding this project, SEHN also envisions the establishment of an Internet commons, where people can name their chosen protectorate and register as guardians. As Carolyn Raffensperger describes it, the Guardianship Project "is a way to name, reshape, and develop appropriate modern applications of ancient roles—the warrior, the guardian—and celebrate and empower those who play these roles in the community."

The Guardianship Project expresses what indigenous wisdom has embodied for centuries: to make decisions with regard for "seven generations to come." The Indigenous Environmental Network (IEN) is a grassroots coalition that has helped to develop this initiative. In its Bemidji Statement of 2006, the IEN brings the following questions to the designation of Guardians for the Seventh Generation:

Who guards this web of life that nurtures and sustains us all?
Who watches out for the land, the sky, the fire, and the water?
Who watches out for our relatives that swim, fly, walk, or crawl?
Who watches out for the plants that are rooted in our Mother Earth?
Who watches out for the life-giving spirits that reside in the underworld?
Who tends the languages of the people and the land?
Who tends the children and the families?
Who tends the peacekeepers in our communities?

The late Walter Bresette, IEN member and a leader of the Anishinaabe nation, had these questions in mind when he drafted a constitutional amendment, granting rights to future beings. He called it the Amendment for the Seventh Generation. It states:

> The right of citizens of the United States to use and enjoy air, water, wildlife, and other renewable resources determined by the Congress to be common property shall not be impaired, nor shall such use impair their availability for the use of future generations.

This would write the protection of the commons into the Constitution, which currently does not include any explicit rights to a clean environment. It's an audacious project but these times require such bold action. As environmental educator David Orr reflects: "It is time for our understanding and refining of that document to be reconciled with our knowledge of natural systems and our growing awareness of obligations and rights that extend broadly throughout the community of life and outward in time as far as the mind dares to imagine."

The Guardianship Project helps us to imagine the kind of world we want to ensure and then to take concrete actions to achieve it. Walter Bresette eloquently evokes the moral imagination we need to safeguard the future:

> As we continue to look for and pick up bundles we left along the wayside, others will help create new bundles for the journey ahead. For sure these steps will be difficult times filled with hardship. But, unless we start now, the future simply will not exist. And, as their scientists report more and more facts, some of us are already dying. Let's join together now, today, and lead the way—the Anishinaabe way. If, as the elders have told us, we are our grandparents' dream, then we must today begin dreaming of our grandchildren.

Fazang and the Three Times

So many opportunities are opening now to play our part in a story that extends through time. As I reflect on this, I am inspired by an ancient teacher of the Dharma. Living fourteen centuries ago, Fazang was a scholar of the Hua Yen scriptures of Mahayana Buddhism. These offer awesomely elaborate descriptions and imagery to convey the Buddha's teaching of dependent co-arising. Vast cosmic scenes spanning all space and time, peopled with astronomical numbers of beings and bodhisattvas, unfold the logic of that teaching to reveal, along with the relatedness of all phenomena, their inter-penetration as well. An image conveying that radical mutuality, like an early promise of today's holographic view of the universe, is the Jeweled Net of Indra. Contemporary scholar Francis Cook describes it this way:

Far away in the heavenly abode of the great god Indra, there is a wonderful net which has been hung by some cunning artificer in such a manner that it stretches out indefinitely in all directions. In accordance with the extravagant tastes of deities, the artificer has hung a single glittering jewel at the net's every node, and since the net itself is infinite in number, the jewels are infinite in number. There hang the jewels, glittering like stars of the first magnitude, a wonderful sight to behold. If we now arbitrarily select one of these jewels for inspection and look closely at it, we will discover that in its polished surface there are reflected all the other jewels in the net, infinite in number. Not only that, but each of the jewels reflected in this one jewel is also reflecting all the other jewels, so that the process of reflection is infinite.

The empress of China was so fascinated by the Hua Yen scriptures that she ordered all eighty volumes to be translated from the Sanskrit. She often came in person to the monastery where the scholars were at work, bringing them food and drink. To celebrate the completion of the project, she invited Master Fazang to the palace to preach about Indra's Net and the inter-penetration of all phenomena. She thanked him for his brilliance and then asked for something more.

"You have explained the teaching to me with great clarity," she said. "Sometimes I can almost see the vast truth of it in my mind's eye. But all this, I realize, is still conjecture." She reminded Fazang of the Buddha's insistence that direct experience was more reliable than inference, and she asked him for an experiential teaching. "Can you give me a demonstration that will reveal the great truth of all-in-one and one-in-all?"

A few days later Fazang escorted the empress to the demonstration he had prepared for her in one of the palace rooms. Mirrors were fixed to its four walls and corners, as well as the ceiling and floor. Then the scholar placed a small statue of the Buddha in the center of the room with a candle beside it.

"Oh, how marvelous!" cried the empress, beholding in awe the panorama of infinite reflections. And she thanked Fa-Tsang for helping her to know the great teaching not only with her intellect, but with her senses.

Afterwards the empress asked the great scholar if he could show in a similar physical fashion the interplay between past, present, and future. Fazang told her that such a demonstration might be possible to contrive. But it would be more difficult, he said, and he did not have the means at hand.

I want to step through time and tell Fazang that we have managed to achieve it. In the radioactive legacy we have created, we have found a way to apprehend our immediate and unseverable connections with future generations. As Sister Rosalie Bertell pointed out, our present choices have a direct influence on whether beings born eons from today will be of sound mind and body. Our karma, the consequence of our actions, now extends into geological time periods—and even as long as Earth's life span to date, given the half-life of depleted uranium, which is 4.5 billion years.

This fact by itself chills the soul. But as I take it in, I hear Fazang reminding me that dependent co-arising is a two-way street. In the mystery of time, the bonds we forge to future beings can bring them into our lives in ways unforeseen in the linear view. In our actions to serve life on Earth, we can feel them at our side lending strength and counsel.

Sometimes I find myself praying, not only *for* them, but also *to* them. I ask them to help us be faithful in the work that we, their ancestors, have been given to do.

> You live inside us, beings of the future.
> In the spiral ribbons of our cells, you are here.
> In our rage for the burning forests, the poisoned fields,
>   the oil-drowned seals,
> you are here.
> You beat in our hearts through late-night meetings.

You accompany us to clear-cuts and toxic dumps
and the halls of the lawmakers.
It is you who drive our dogged labors to save what is left.

O you, who will walk this Earth when we are gone,
    stir us awake.
Behold through our eyes the beauty of this world.
Let us feel your breath in our lungs, your cry in our throat.
Let us see you in the poor, the homeless, the sick.
Haunt us with your hunger, hound us with your claims,
that we may honor the life that links us.

You have as yet no faces we can see, no names we can say.
But we need only hold you in our mind, and you teach us
    patience.
You attune us to measures of time where healing can happen,
where soil and souls can mend.
You reveal courage within us we had not suspected,
love we had not owned.
O you who come after, help us remember: we are your
    ancestors.
Fill us with gladness for the work that must be done.

REFERENCE NOTES

All scriptural quotes are from the Pali Text Society editions.

Page

CHAPTER ONE

23 "The lover . . . particle." Jnaneshwar, Andrew Harvey, *The Return of the Mother*. New Zealand: Penguin Group, 2004.

24 "Through the calculations . . ." Italo Calvino, *Cosmicomics*. New York: Harcourt Brace Jovanovich, 1968, pp.43–47.

27 "I am a feather . . . I am alive." Natachee Scott Momaday, http://www.poemhunter.com/i/ebooks/pdf/natachee_scott_momaday_2004_9.pdf

28 "Being rock, . . . died." Thich Nhat Hanh, *The Collected Poems of Thich Nhat Hanh*. Berkeley: Parallax Press, 1992.

CHAPTER TWO

31 "they who . . ." *Majjhima Nikaya* II.32.

31 "Coming to be . . ." *Digha Nikaya* II.33.

32 "I have penetrated this truth . . ." Ibid., II.36.

33 "There are those . . . understand." Ibid., II.37–39.

33 "This being. . . ceases." *Samyutta Nikaya* II.28, 65; *Majjhima Nikaya* II.32, etc.

34 "Wonderful, lord . . . faring on." *Digha Nikaya* II.91.

35 "Is sensory experience. . ." Thomas S. Kuhn, *The Structure of Scientific Revolutions*. Chicago: University of Chicago Press, 1970, p. 126.

36 "Were a man . . ." *Samyutta Nikaya* III.57.

37 "Whatever is . . . ," *Anguttara Nikaya* II.24.

39 "two sheaves . . . would fall." *Samyutta Nikaya* II.103, 113.

39 "kidneys . . . urine." *Digha Nikaya* II.293.

39 "Grasping at things . . ." *Digha Nikaya* II.1.

39 "turned on me . . . abundance." *Majjhima Nikaya* I.247.

CHAPTER THREE

44 "Ah, the savor of it!" *Digha Nikaya* III.86.

45 "to be . . . censured." Ibid., II.93.

46 "the vulgar . . . menials." Ibid., III.82.

47 "So long . . . prosper." Ibid., II.77.

49 "those men . . . realm." Ibid., I.135.

50 "Moreover I have . . . Dhamma." Lucien Stryk, *World of the Buddha*. New York: Doubleday Anchor, 1968, p. 245 (Seventh Pillar Edict of Asoka).

51 "Wherever there are . . . " P. Wheelwright, ed. and tr., *Aristotle: Natural Science, Psychology, and Nichomachean Ethics.* New York: Odyssey Press, 1935, p. 35.

52 "glorious . . .," *Vinaya,* I.113.

CHAPTER FOUR

55 "Did I live . . ." *Samyutta Nikaya* II.26.

55 "Where others . . . 'action,'" T.W. Rhys Davids, *Dialogues of the Buddha (Digha Nikaya).* London: Pali Text Society, 1973, II, p. 189.

56 "This body . . . feelings." *Samyutta Nikaya* II.62.

56 "My action. . . refuge." H. Oldenburg, *Buddha: His Life, His Doctrine, His Order.* Delhi: Indological Book House, 1971, p. 243.

57 "The idea . . . exhausted." Lama Anagarika Govinda, *The Psychological Attitude of Early Buddhist Philosophy.* New York: Samuel Weiser, Inc., 1971, pp. 56–57.

57 "neither the . . . verity." *Anguttara Nikaya* I.174.

57 "Where there . . . deeds." *Samyutta Nikaya* II.38.

58 "intent on vigilence. . . mindfulness aroused." *Majjhima Nikaya* I.32.

58 "Wherefore . . . going." *Samyutta Nikaya* II.264.

59 "Thanks to . . . past." Karl Deutsch, "Toward a Cybernetic Model of Man and Society," Walter Buckley, ed., *Modern Systems Research for the Behavioral Scientist,* (Chicago, IL: Aldine Publishing Co., 1968) p.397.

59 "Each of us . . . Salvation." Ibid., p. 398.

59 "It sees . . . decisions." Ibid., p. 398–399.

60 "The eternal . . . 'intentions.'" O.H. Mowrer, "Ego Psychology, Cybernetics, and Learning Theory," Buckley, op. cit., p. 338.

CHAPTER FIVE

67 "to the Indian mind . . . dimension." A.K. Coomaraswamy, "Kha and Other Words Denoting Zero in Connection with the Metaphysics of Space," *Bulletin of the School of Oriental Studies,* London Institution, Vol. VII, Part 3, 1934, p. 496.

68 "Garlic . . . beginning." T.S. Eliot, *Four Quartets.* Orlando, FL: Harcourt, Inc., 1971.

70 "with her . . . ," Richard Lannoy, *The Speaking Tree.* Oxford: Oxford University Press, 1971, p. 107.

CHAPTER SIX

77 *Learning from the Onondaga,* www.onondaganation.org

79 "The people . . . one." *The Mohawk Thanksgiving Prayer,* medicinecrow.net/ThanksGiving.html

83 "I want . . . love." Drew Dellinger, *love letter to the milky way: a book of poems.* Poets for Global Justice, drewdellinger.org.

85 For more information regarding the spiral in group work, Joanna Macy, Molly Young, Brown, *Coming Back to Life: Practices to Reconnect Our Lives, Our World.* New Society Publishers, 1998, p.71.

86 "Then all . . . turn." Rainer Maria Rilke, translated by Anita Barrows and Joanna Macy, *Rilke's Book of Hours: Love Poems to God.* NY: Riverhead Books, 1996.

CHAPTER SEVEN
87 "short-tailed albatross . . . wolf." *IUCN Red List of Endangered Species*, www.iucnredlist. org

CHAPTER EIGHT
96 "essentially . . . creative." Kazimierz Dabrowski. *Positive Disintegration,* Boston: Little Brown & Co., 1964.
96 "but whirlpools . . . themselves," Norbert Wiener. *Human Use of Human Beings. Cybernetics and Society.* New York: Avon Books, 1967.
99 "whistle-blowing . . . lives." Daniel Ellsberg. *The Truth-Telling Project,* www.ellsberg.net
100 "The ability . . . hope." William Lynch. *Images of Hope: Imagination as Healer of the Hopeless.* University of Notre Dame Press, 1979.
101 "For there . . . order." Jacob Needleman. *A Sense of the Cosmos: The Encounter of Modern Science and Ancient Truth.* Dutton, 1977.
102 "Quiet friend . . . I am." Rainer Maria Rilke, translated by Anita Barrows and Joanna Macy, Rilke's *Book of Hours: Love Poems to God.* NY: Riverhead Books, 1996.

CHAPTER NINE
107 "We are . . . inter-penetration." Paul Shepard with Daniel McKinley. *Subversive Science: Essays toward an Ecology of Man.* Boston: Houghton Mifflin, 1969.
108 "When humans . . . dancing." John Seed, Joanna Macy, Pat Flemming, Arne Naess. *Thinking Like a Mountain: Towards a Council of All Beings.* New Society Publishers, 1988.

CHAPTER THIRTEEN
146 "I entered . . . ecstasy." Tim Hunt, ed. *The Collected Poetry of Robinson Jeffers.* Stanford: Stanford University Press, Vol. l, l988.

CHAPTER FOURTEEN
151 "We have . . . competition." Robert Bellah, Richard Madsen, William Sullivan, Ann Swindler, and Steven Tipton. *Habits of the Heart: Individualism and Commitment in American Life.* Berkeley, CA: University of California Press, 1996.
153 "the total . . . deciding." Gregory Bateson. *Steps to an Ecology of Mind.* New York: Ballantine Books, 1972.
154 "this false . . . symbiotic." Ibid.
156 "where the . . . world." Arne Naess. "Self-Realization" in *Thinking Like a Mountain: Towards a Council of All Beings.* New Society Publishers, 1988.
156 "In this . . . selves." Ibid.

CHAPTER SIXTEEN
174 "this spilling . . . forever." Tyrone Cashman. Unpublished manuscript, 1989.
174 "We need not . . . severance." Robert J. Lifton. *The Broken Connection.* New York: Simon and Schuster, 1979, p. 338.
175 "When the . . . do that." Cashman, op. cit.
177 "Our perceptions . . . cancer." Larry Dossey, M.D. *Space Time and Medicine.* Boulder: Shambhala Publications, Inc., 1982, p. 49.

177 "My teacher . . . faster." Ariane Barth. "Im Reisswolf der Geschwindigkeit" ("In the Wolf Fangs of Speed"). Der Spiegel, Nov. 20, 1989, p. 210–214.

180 "It's all . . . manner." Thomas Berry. *The Dream of the Earth*. San Francisco: Sierra Club, 1988, p. 123.

190 "heal itself . . . again." Jeremy Rifkin. *Time Wars: The primary conflict in human history*. New York: Henry Holt and Company, 1987.

CHAPTER SEVENTEEN

196 *The Precautionary Principle*, The Science and Environmental Health Network, www.sehn.org

198 "Who . . . communities," The Indigenous Environmental Network, www.ienearth.org

198 "The right . . . generations." Walter Bresette, Anishinaabe Nation, www.protecttheearth.net

198 " It is . . . imagine." David W. Orr, *The Law of the Land,* Orion Magazine, January/February 2004.

199 "As we . . . grandchildren." Walter Bresette, www.ienearth.org

199 "Far away . . . infinite." Francis Cook. The Avatamsaka Sutra. *Hua-Yen Buddhism: The Jewel Net of Indra,* Pennsylvania State University, 1977.

201 "You live . . . done." Joanna Macy. *Prayers for a Thousand Years*, Elisabeth Roberts and Elias Amidon, ed., Harper San Francisco, 1999.

Acknowledgments

Some material for this book appeared previously, in a different version, in the following sources:

Chapter 1: World as Lover, World as Self
Adapted from the Viriditas Lecture on Spiritual Values and Contemporary Issues, sponsored by Friends of Creation Spirituality (Berkeley, CA, November 1987).

Chapter 5: Mother of All Buddhas
This piece first appeared in *Anima Magazine* (Fall 1976).

Chapter 7: The Bestiary
This chapter is an updated version of the original piece that appeared in *Thinking Like a Mountain* (Philadelphia, PA: New Society Publishers, 1988).

Chapter 8: Despair Work
An early form of this chapter first appeared as the booklet *Despair Work* (Philadelphia, PA: New Society Publishers, 1981).

Chapter 9: Faith, Power, and Ecology
This chapter draws inspiration and structure from Joanna's Schumacher Lecture in Bristol, UK, 1986.

Chapter 12: Taking Heart
Four of these meditations appear in shorter form in *Despair and Personal Power in the Nuclear Age* (Philadelphia, PA: New Society Publishers, 1983), Chapter Eight.

Chapter 14: The Greening of the Self
Adapted from a lecture at Colorado University (January 1989) and subsequently published in *Dharma Gaia* (Berkeley: Parallax Press, 1990), pp. 53-63.

Chapter 16: To Reinhabit Time
Adapted from a presentation at the Conference on the Post-Modern Presidency (Santa Barbara, CA, July 1989).

Chapter 17: In League with the Beings of the Future
An earlier form of this chapter first appeared in *Creation Magazine*.

**PARALLAX
PRESS**

Parallax Press is a nonprofit publisher, founded and inspired by Zen Master Thich Nhat Hanh. We publish books on mindfulness in daily life and are committed to making these teachings accessible to everyone and preserving them for future generations. We do this work to alleviate suffering and contribute to a more just and joyful world.

Parallax Press
P.O. Box 7355
Berkeley, CA 94707
parallax.org

Monastics and laypeople practice the art of mindful living in the tradition of Thich Nhat Hanh at retreat communities worldwide. To reach any of these communities, or for information about individuals and familes joining for a practice period, please contact:

Plum Village
13 Martineau
33580 Dieulivol, France
plumvillage.org

Magnolia Grove Monastery
123 Towles Rd.
Batesville, MS 38606
magnoliagrovemonastery.org

Blue Cliff Monastery
3 Minefulness Road
Pine Bush, NY 12566
bluecliffmonastery.org

Deer Park Monastery
2499 Melru Lane
Escondido, CA 92026
deerparkmonastery.org

The Mindfulness Bell, a journal of the art of mindful living in the tradition of Thich Nhat Hanh, is published three times a year by Plum Village. To subscribe or to see the worldwide directory of Sanghas, visit
mindfulnessbell.org